Learning to
Manage Conflict

Learning to Manage Conflict

Getting People to Work Together Productively

Dean Tjosvold

LEXINGTON BOOKS
An Imprint of Macmillan, Inc.
New York

Maxwell Macmillan Canada
Toronto

Maxwell Macmillan International
New York   Oxford   Singapore   Sydney

Library of Congress Cataloging-in-Publication Data

Tjosvold, Dean.
  Learning to manage conflict: getting people to work together
productively / Dean Tjosvold.
      p.   cm.
    ISBN 0-02-932491-2
  1. Conflict management.   2. Interpersonal relations.   I. Title.
  HD42.T583   1993
  650.1'3—dc20   92-38942
                                                         CIP

Lexington Books
An Imprint of Macmillan, Inc.
866 Third Avenue, New York, N.Y. 10022

Maxwell Macmillan Canada, Inc.
1200 Eglinton Avenue East
Suite 200
Don Mills, Ontario M3C 3N1

Macmillan, Inc. is part of the Maxwell Communication Group of Companies.

Printed in the United States of America

printing number
1 2 3 4 5 6 7 8 9 10

To Jason, Wesley, Lena, and Colleen

I rely on their glorious laughter and exhilarating conflicts

Contents

PART FOUR

Reaching Out

Preface

Learning to Manage Conflict describes how you and your colleagues, family members, and friends can strengthen your abilities to deal with the differences that threaten to divide you. It shows how you can use your arguments, disputes, and frustrations to deepen your competence and relationships. You will see how well-managed conflict helps us reach out to others and enrich our thinking so that we solve problems creatively, accomplish the extraordinary, and live and work together with acceptance and respect. This book will give you the tools to manage conflicts with colleagues, family, and bosses productively.

Conflict, though it can cause distress and prevent you from getting your way, is not an inevitably destructive and imposing barrier you would be better off without. Wishing we could live without conflicts and avoiding discussing them are the real barriers. Managing conflict is an essential life skill that is too often neglected. Considerable research has documented that well-managed, cooperative conflict contributes to the productivity and innovativeness of organizations and the competence and well-being of people. Managing conflict is so vital today that it is a "must know."

For Work and Family

Work and family are often considered distinct worlds that compete for our loyalty. Our relationships in organizations are to be formal and task-oriented; those in families, emotional and intimate. But we cannot divide ourselves in half and live two separate lives. We have strong feelings and attitudes at work and they affect our relationships off the job. Too often organizations have reinforced conflict-negative habits and left people frustrated and unprepared to deal with their family conflicts.

Dealing directly and cooperatively with conflict is as critical for a nurturing family as for a productive organization. This book focuses on using experiences in organizations to develop conflict competence to counteract the negative learning given in traditional organizations. But our family conflicts can also benefit from the issue-oriented, problem-solving approach associated with business.

Ironically, our need to manage conflict helps us integrate our personal and professional lives. Although we discuss different issues at different levels, we can use the idea of cooperative conflict to forge more credible and effective ways of dealing with our disagreements and fights at work and at home.

Learning Is Practical

How practical is learning to manage conflict? People are so distracted by the diversions of contemporary life and organizations so pressured by competition to perform and speed their products to the marketplace that learning seems like a luxury few people and organizations can afford. Crises demand survival in the short term, not learning for the long-term. We are conditioned to get through conflicts to get on with business. But, as we will discover, well-managed conflict is necessary to get important jobs done. Learning to manage conflict is an investment in our future productivity and innovation.

Yet conflicts have been so much avoided and so badly managed in many organizations and families that people are hostile and suspicious. They see each other as too arrogant, too manipulative, or too vulnerable to deal directly and usefully with their differences. With such attitudes, trying to improve conflict management may seem too idealistic and doomed to failure. But learning to manage conflict is a practical way to break away from old working habits and build healthy, productive relationships.

After recognizing the costs of their unproductive conflict handling, antagonistic and suspicious coworkers, or spouses, can work on how they express their anger and deal with frustration. They have a common task and cooperative interests in learning. As people help each other discuss their conflicts, they have concrete evidence that others are not as arrogant and as vulnerable as previously assumed, and they recognize their ability to work together. As they improve their conflict management, they strengthen their confidence in each other and in themselves. They can integrate their views to solve problems and combine their efforts to reach goals.

Moving away from this competitive, short-term focus to a cooperative, long-term orientation of continuous improvement requires insight and determination. It does not, however, require perfection. We cannot expect ourselves and our conflict partners to handle conflicts flawlessly. But we can realistically commit ourselves to learning.

Conflict to Manage Change

Change begets conflict, conflict begets change. Families debate whether they should move from their recently commercialized city neighborhood to suburbia. People debate their environmental impact and discuss how to adjust lifestyles.

In organizations, people disagree about how they can use a new technology; they argue over how to cope with a shrinking, competitive market and take advantage of a growing one. Though trained and oriented into different specializations and professions, people are required to work together to develop, manufacture, and market profitable new products in an intensely competitive marketplace. Organizations are confronted with a host of conflicts as they try to make joint ventures and other cooperative strategies work.

New international trade agreements require countries to resolve conflicts to establish fair trade, rethink political sovereignty, and realign their economies to realize the benefits of trade. The end of the Cold War does not mean the beginning of an era of harmony, but requires that people from the East and West forge new ways of working and living together.

Learning to manage conflict is a critical investment in improving how we, our families, and our organizations adapt and take advantage of change. Managing conflicts well does not insulate us from change, nor does it mean that we will always come out on top or get all that we want. However, effective conflict management helps us keep in touch with new developments and create solutions appropriate for new threats and opportunities.

Much evidence shows we have often failed to manage our conflicts and respond to change effectively. High divorce rates, disheartening examples of sexual and physical abuse of children, the expensive failures of international joint ventures, and bloody ethnic violence have convinced many people that we do not have the abilities to cope with our complex interpersonal, organizational, and global conflicts.

Our attempts to get by rather than manage our conflicts have left our families, organizations, and societies in disarray. In every year of the 1980s, more than 1 million American children saw their parents divorce. Despite the emphasis on developing excellent companies that serve customers, U.S. employees, according to several polls, became more mistrustful of management in the 1980s. They wanted stronger relationships and more involvement, but thought they got less honesty.

Not only do we have relentless change and conflict, but we must deal with our conflicts under new conditions. Job and geographical mobility—nearly twenty percent of U.S. households move every year—means that people must manage conflicts with people they do not know. Because of strong immigration and high rates of female and minority entry into the workforce, women and nonwhites are expected to be eighty-five percent of the additions to the U.S. workforce until the year 2000.

Contemporary organizations demand that conflicts be resolved efficiently under tight time pressures. In addition to the challenges to domestic business brought by rapid immigration, international cooperative business strategies and the global marketplace put us in conflict with people with different cultures, ways of communicating, and approaches to problems.

We can use conflict management knowledge to help us repair our fragmented families, groups and organizations. Our families and work groups need to become more effective at managing conflicts to become more united and supportive. Unity is not decreed or imposed, but worked out through honest discussion. The theory of cooperative conflict is a common framework that diverse people can learn and apply together to deal with emerging conflicts.

The Book's Agenda

Learning to Manage Conflict will help you build upon your strengths to tackle difficult conflicts. It is for people who are looking for an alternative to getting by through short-term crisis management. In the following pages, you will learn to manage conflicts with colleagues, family, and friends more honestly and productively.

The book has four parts. The first part, "Facing the Challenge," shows how together we can understand the imperative to manage conflict and the option to manage conflict cooperatively. The second part, "Laying The Foundations for Learning," describes the ideas and relationships that facilitate developing conflict abilities and sensitivities. The third part, "Extending Conflict Competence," challenges us to learn to put the intellectual, emotional, and interest sides of conflict to work. Part Four, "Reaching Out," reminds us that we want to empower our conflict partners so that we can manage our conflicts cooperatively.

The Drama of Conflict

Conflict is such a rich phenomenon that it is a major industry. Newspaper, television, and radio news reporters present and analyze conflicts in the neighborhood, debates in the state legislature, struggles between groups and regions, global trade wars, and world political alignments. Talk show hosts use controversy to explore issues and raise their ratings. Violence and "good guys against bad guys" plots are time-honored ways to sell movies. Fiction writers create conflicts that invite us to probe ourselves and our relationships.

But this industry is geared to escalating and destructive conflict. The attention that we give to cooperative conflict and to managing it well is, by comparison, a cottage industry—although with growth potential. Compared to coverage of explosive conflict, writing about conflict management can appear dry and removed from our experiences. Even the word *conflict* seems distant from our fights and arguments and rivalries. The centrality and pervasiveness of conflict can make facing it and understanding its complexities difficult. How can we apply elegant, relatively simple ideas to cope with such a multisided, emotional experience as conflict and its management?

I have developed a story with characters and dialogue to help you see how the book's ideas and suggestions apply to concrete situations and to close the gap between what you read here and what you can do in your life. The people are fictitious, but they and their conflicts are based on actual people and situations I have encountered as a consultant, therapist, employee, family member, business owner, educator, and researcher.

Your conflicts are, of course, different from those of the people you will meet in the following chapters, and you may have to be more patient and persistent to improve your abilities to handle conflict. We usually find our own conflicts more complex and difficult than other people's. It can seem so easy to analyze and decide how our friends should deal with their conflicts, yet we feel paralyzed when contemplating our own. I hope that you and your partners will study the book's ideas and examples and together create ways of making your conflicts cooperative and productive.

PART ONE

Facing the Challenge

The fact that a problem will certainly take a long time to solve, and that it will demand the attention of many minds for several generations, is no justification for postponing the study. And, in times of emergency, it may prove in the long run that the problems we have postponed or ignored, rather than those we have failed to attack successfully, will return to plague us. Our difficulties of the moment must always be dealt with somehow; but our permanent difficulties are difficulties of every moment.

—*T.S. Eliot*

Much is possible when we manage our conflicts, but we must be sensitive, determined, and skillful. Chapter 1 reviews the value of learning to managing conflict, basic processes of learning, and criteria for constructive conflict. Chapter 2 illustrates that, in addition to frustrating problem solving and disrupting relationships, poorly managed conflict reinforces stereotypes and biases that get in the way of effective future conflict management. But managing conflict effectively offers a way for us to learn more useful lessons about conflict and working with others. Chapter 3 shows how cooperative conflict can help us examine and strengthen how we approach conflict.

1

Moving Toward Cooperative Conflict

Where there is much desire to learn, there of necessity will be much arguing, much writing, many opinions; for opinion in good men is but knowledge in the making.

—John Milton

People debate opposing views, negotiate different agendas, and express their frustrations about many issues in many ways. Unfortunately, what they seldom disagree about is their desire to avoid conflict. But conflict itself does not destroy; it is avoidance and other destructive ways of handling important conflicts that undermine our well-being, confidence, and effectiveness.

Too often we avoid discussing our differences to try to get by. We hope an arrogant boss will soften; when he does not, we complain to colleagues, withdraw from work, and look for a job elsewhere. We expect an insensitive family member to know what we need; when she does not, we explode in anger or walk away in despair. We seek new relationships, but find ourselves repeating old habits and getting embroiled in familiar conflicts.

The habit of avoiding conflict, interrupted with outbursts of shouting and fighting, exacerbates our dilemmas and reinforces the cycle of destructive conflict. Rather than develop the sensitivities, skills, and confidence to confront new difficulties and conflicts, we feel overwhelmed and resign ourselves to the idea that avoidance—either by our own silence or by threatening others into silence—is our only avenue.

But improving how we deal with conflict, as this chapter shows, is a practical investment for ourselves, our friends and colleagues, and our organizations. This chapter also describes the processes by which people can strengthen their conflict abilities and identifies the criteria of successful conflict.

Conflict's Benefits

Problem awareness. Discussing frustrations identifies poor quality, excessive costs, injustices, and other barriers to effectiveness.

Improved solutions. Debating opposing views digs into issues, searches for information and insight, and integrates ideas to create solutions responsive to several perspectives.

Productivity. Managed conflict reduces the time wasted by brooding and redoing tasks and results in more efficient use of resources.

Organizational change. Conflict creates incentives to challenge and change outmoded procedures, assignments, and structures.

Personal development. Confronting conflicts teaches managers and employees how their style affects others and reveals the competencies they need to develop.

Knowledge and creativity. Elaboration and listening help people retain ideas and understand their implications. They become more creative as they explore alternatives and integrate different points of view.

Awareness. Knowing what people are willing to fight about keeps them in touch with each other. People learn what makes themselves and others irritated and angry and what is important to them.

Self-acceptance. Expressing frustrations and important feelings helps people accept and value themselves. Having others listen and respond to their feelings builds people's self-esteem.

Psychological maturity. Addressing conflicts encourages people to take the perspectives of others and become less egocentric. They feel confident and empowered to cope with difficulties by dealing directly with them.

Morale. Discussion and problem solving help employees release their tensions and stress. They feel confident that they have faced difficulties together and their relationships are strong and open.

Challenge and fun. The stimulation, arousal, and involvement of conflict can be enjoyable, and can be a welcome break from monotony for employees. It invites people to examine and appreciate the intricacies of their relationships.

The Imperative to Learn

Enduring achievement requires managing conflict. Competent professionals, dedicated managers, and aggressive business people confront many obstacles and frustrations that must be dealt with to succeed. The most important involve families, friends, and colleagues, who may obstruct their efforts and get in their way or help them overcome barriers and solve problems.

Without conflict management, lasting accomplishment is elusive. Employees wait for an opportunity to undo and undermine their dictatorial boss. The hard-driving entrepreneur faces the prospect of his estranged children selling off the family business and fighting over the spoils. Without the give and take of productive conflict, relationships remain shallow, problems unexamined, and commitment to decisions superficial.

Learning to manage conflict facilitates the competence and well-being of people as well as the effectiveness of organizations. Through cooperative conflict, managers recognize shortcomings in their present strategies, experiment with new approaches, and get feedback and support to refine their leadership abilities. Production employees express their views and learn more about marketing by understanding the diverse perspectives of marketing specialists and customers at the same time that marketers learn about their colleagues' priorities. Cooperative conflict integrates personal needs for individuality and fulfillment with organizational requirements for productivity and innovation.

The Learning Organization

Accelerating change in markets, technologies, and people has made managers interested in continuous improvement and the "learning organization." Maintaining the status quo is no longer acceptable; the advantages of a new technology, new product, or new market are increasingly temporary. Organizations must continually adapt to changes and exploit emerging opportunities. People must upgrade and refine their abilities or be left behind.

Becoming more effective at managing conflict is fundamental to becoming a organization that learns and prospers. A company does not continue to serve its customers with high-quality products by simply talking about how they are quality people who care about their customers. It takes the hard work of conflict management. Marketing, production, and research and development must come together to discuss various ideas to add value to products, production employees must hammer out how they can improve processes to reduce errors, and front-line people must know how to respond to customer complaints and ideas. It is through conflict that the organization keeps in touch with its customers, suppliers, and employees.

By improving the way they manage their conflict, people strengthen their relationships, guide an organization's adaptation, and improve individual competence. Poorly managed conflicts divide people and leave them unwilling and unable to assist and stimulate each other to learn. Escalating conflicts can even threaten a company's survival.

Barriers to Learning

The vital importance of learning does not make it automatically happen. There are many barriers to learning in traditional organizations. Managers and professionals are expected to demonstrate their competence; they are tough-minded winners who are in charge of the situation. Many organizations move in and out of crises where the emphasis is on getting the immediate job done, not on long-term learning. Ineffective relationships very much interfere. People knowledgeable about markets are aligned against those who can change the company's products.

The most popular answer to why so many important conflicts are mismanaged is lack of motivation. Despite the benefits of cooperative conflict, people see more advantage to themselves in trying to win or avoid the conflict. More often, though, the problem is not motivation. Many people deal much better with minor conflicts than with vital ones. People often want to manage their conflicts constructively, but do not have the abilities and confidence to do so.

Organizations have greatly underinvested in their relationships and in their conflict management abilities. They have believed they could invest in a new technology, develop and market a new product, and become more participative without much attention to conflict. But learning to manage conflict complements these investments and is a foundation for ongoing improvement.

Strengthening Your Abilities

You need both ideas and experience to improve your conflict management. Ideas without practice remain elusive and misunderstood. Without ideas, people repeat old mistakes and fail to see alternatives. It is through ongoing experimenting that you acquire the savvy to analyze your situation, decide what you want to do, and carry out your plans.

Cooperative, growth-oriented relationships are critical for this continuous learning. You get entangled into conflict together with others; you can best get untangled together. You and your conflict partners can discuss ideas and then together practice new approaches. You can give each other the feedback and support necessary for real change and growth. Learning to manage conflict, like managing conflict itself, is too challenging to do alone; it is much better done cooperatively.

Using Valid Theory

A useful, valid conflict theory is critical to diagnosing our present attitudes and approaches and to understanding how we can improve our conflict management. Unfortunately, people have various, often misleading, theories about conflict.

Defining Conflict

Perhaps the most obstructive idea is that conflict occurs because people have opposing interests. In this view, conflict inevitably means that people are working against each other; what one wants is incompatible with what another wants; their goals are competitive; what one gets comes at the expense of others. The best that can be accomplished is a compromise where each gives up in order to receive something.

A much more useful definition, based on the work of Morton Deutsch of Columbia University, is that conflict involves incompatible behaviors; one person is interfering, disrupting, or in some other way making another's actions less effective. While this difference may seem minor and academic, it has vast practical implications.

People with compatible, cooperative interests can be in conflict as they argue about the best means to accomplish their common tasks, distribute the benefits and burdens of their cooperative effort, and determine how they are to treat each other. Husband and wife both want the best vacation for the family, but disagree on whether it should be a car or a bike trip. Task force members all want to improve company profitability, but some want to market the product now and others to redevelop it. They may be irritated that others are not listening to their views carefully enough. Our studies suggest that within organizations most conflicts occur when people have cooperative interests. People can reach their goals when others also reach theirs; they must be successful together.

The assumption that conflict is based on opposing interests leads to viewing conflict as a struggle to see whose strength and interests will dominate and whose will be subordinated. We must fight to win, or at least not lose. The assumption that you have largely cooperative goals leads to viewing the conflict as a common problem to be solved for mutual benefit, which in turn makes it more likely that the conflict will be constructive and that people will improve their abilities to deal with conflict.

Cooperative Conflict Theory

Cooperative conflict theory is elegant and powerful. It suggests the kind of relationship that partners in conflict want to establish as well as the actions that complement these relationships. When people believe their goals are cooperative ("We are in this together." "We swim or sink together."), they are committed to promoting each other and helping each other be effective ("We trust and rely

upon each other."). Then they are prepared to consider each other's ideas and try to combine them into a mutually beneficial solution. They use the conflict to get the job done and strengthen their relationship.

Studies show that cooperative conflict builds people up, strengthens their relationships, and gets things done. Cooperative conflict is a practical way to integrate the needs of people and the requirements of work.

Breaking away from Competitive Conflict

A major obstacle to applying the theory is that in many organizations, groups, and families, people assume that others believe conflict is inevitably competitive. They see "strong" members as aggressive, stubborn, arrogant, closed-minded, and determined to win. They see "weak" members as too passive, coy, and fragile to be open and face losing a conflict. Although they are willing to deal directly and helpfully with problems and differences, they assume others are committed to winning or to avoiding. These attitudes and assumptions make productive conflict very difficult, even improbable. While learning to manage conflict is useful when a conflict partner is unwilling to change, the most powerful impact occurs when people learn to manage conflict together.

Conflict partners can work together to move away from competitive ideas and habits to create a cooperative conflict team and organization. Discussing the benefits of cooperative conflict and the price each side is paying for the destructive conflict can convince them to invest in improving their abilities to deal with conflict. Then they can study cooperative conflict to understand how it is an alternative to viewing conflict as a competitive fight over opposing interests.

People can commit themselves publicly to managing their conflicts openly and cooperatively. Although they realize that they cannot transform their ways of working overnight, they can credibly convey that they are motivated to learn cooperative ways of managing conflict. In this way, team members move away from seeing each other as arrogant or passive to believing that others are direct, open-minded, and responsive people who want to manage their differences.

People need to follow this commitment with action to put cooperative values, procedures, and skills in place. The team identifies the rules for discussing conflicts and problems, allocates bonuses and other rewards, and undertakes the training that will support them in handling conflicts cooperatively. They agree they have a right to speak their minds and to disagree with each other. This book describes procedures and processes people can use to learn and develop their skills.

Conflict partners should strive for ongoing development and improvement. They should study cooperative conflict, rededicate themselves to learning, and help each other refine their abilities and skills. Learning to manage conflict is a continuous journey, not a one-stop trip.

Limitations of Cooperative Conflict

This book addresses the serious underuse of cooperative conflict in our organizations and families. But I do not believe that cooperative conflict is the only viable approach to conflict. You want alternatives so that you can chose when and how you are going to conflict.

Sometimes cooperative conflict is not desirable. Interests can be highly competitive: a protagonist insists that we do something we consider illegal, unethical, or contrary to our basic interests. At times we have to refuse to negotiate and must get our way. When we don't have to work or live with another in the future, it may be prudent to get as much as we can for ourselves.

Cooperative conflict can be impractical. Sometimes a crisis requires decisive, unilateral action. Sometimes conflicts must be avoided because people are too stressed and unskilled. Many conflicts are too minor to warrant much investment in the demands of give-and-take conflict. Few people relish arguing continually over small issues but would rather accommodate, compromise or flip a coin. Spouses take turns selecting the news program; one sibling cuts the cookie in two and the other choses.

Yet biases easily interfere with making practical choices about how to approach conflict. Some organizations always shout crisis to avoid open discussion of conflicts. However, a recent study documented that captains, copilots, and flight attendants dealt with threats to the safety of their airplane more effectively through cooperative, open discussion than by unilateral decision making.

Perhaps the most misleading reason for not using cooperative conflict is the belief that it requires unlimited resources, while resources are scarce. However, scarce resources can also strengthen cooperative goals. In companies under fire to make money, marketing and production departments recognize more clearly that they must pull together to produce and market profitable products. Even budget conflicts often place people in cooperation. A research and development department cannot expect to be funded properly in the long term without successful production and marketing departments.

Cooperative conflict becomes more viable as our conflict partners become more important to us and as we take a long-term view of our interests. If we win a conflict with a colleague, she will not be a valuable ally in the future. If we win a conflict with a family member, he will be less likely to support us. However, even with people important to us, some conflicts will be avoided, some compromised, and some won. In effective teams and families, people recognize that overall they are committed to managing their conflicts for mutual benefit but are practical and flexible enough to accommodate, fight, avoid and use other approaches.

Criteria for Successful Conflict

We are about to embark on the interesting, challenging effort to acquire the ideas, sensitivities, and skills to manage diverse conflict. We explore how managing conflict is critical for developing constructive relationships. We dig into the idea of constructive, cooperative conflict and see its implications. We examine our assumptions and look for biases.

The aim of this book is to stimulate your thinking and develop your learning so that you have the abilities, procedures, and confidence to manage your conflicts. You can use the information in this book not just to end one conflict but to become more skillful for other present and future conflicts. But what is the aim of managing conflict? How do you know when you are becoming more effective at managing conflict?

Agreement

It is easy to assume that goal of managing conflict is to get an agreement, to make a deal, and to end the conflict efficiently and effectively. We usually do not want to hang on to our conflicts; rather, we try to put them behind us so that they do not reappear in a different, potentially more destructive form. We also want to use our time and resources efficiently; we don't want to invest thousands on a small conflict.

But reaching a valid agreement efficiently is not the only and not always the most salient criteria. We do not want to reach agreements that leave us vulnerable and exploited. We should know our best alternatives to reaching an agreement. Agreements may preclude seeking more valuable opportunities elsewhere. Agreements that simply paper over differences are likely to leave us frustrated and stifled.

Relationships

Strengthening our relationships with our conflict partners is often a more reliable measure of effective conflict management. Agreements that damage the relationship usually are not very useful and may be worse than no agreement. Without strong relationships, agreements may not be implemented. If the discussion strengthens the relationship, it is more likely that future discussions can develop a richer and more successful resolution of the conflict.

But a strengthened relationship is not a certain criteria either. Sometimes the best resolution is to end the relationship. In some cases, marriage partners do not have the motivation, abilities, and endurance necessary to deal with their many conflicts. We want the best automobile for our money and care much less about our relationship with the salesperson.

Learning

Learning from managing conflict is a consistent criteria of successful conflict management. We have used the conflict to become more aware of ourselves and others; we feel more able to solve problems; we believe we can reach useful agreements and establish productive, enjoyable relationships; our relationships are stronger and more able to deal with future difficulties; we feel more in control of our lives.

As we manage our conflicts, we become more effective. It can be reassuring—especially in the heat, antagonism, and despair of tough conflicts—to remember that we can use this conflict to learn.

Becoming more effective at managing conflict gives much but requires much. You are more able to manage conflict when you and your conflict partners have a clear understanding and conviction that, though you disagree, you have cooperative goals. You must also sharpen your communication and listening skills so that you are open with your ideas and feelings as you open-mindedly consider others' ideas. Yet there are imposing confusions, suspicions, and other pitfalls to becoming more effective. The next chapter shows how the competitive-avoiding approach frustrates conflict management and reinforces biases and barriers.

2

Learning from Conflict

Have you learned lessons only of those who admired you, and were tender with you, and stood aside for you?
Have you not learned great lessons from those who braced themselves against you, and disputed the passage with you?
—Walt Whitman

Eric and Willem Fight at NorTel

"You expect me to believe that the reason you want your way is because we're suppose to serve customers and act as a team? " Willem Mulder, manager of the Market Support Department at NorTel, said in disbelief. His anger pushed these words out and, though he stopped short of losing his temper, he worried that these words left him vulnerable. He doubted he could be so direct with Eric.

Eric Kessel, sales manager at NorTel, was angry that Willem was again obstructing a sale by throwing bureaucratic obstacles in its path. "Look, it's not my way that we're talking about. It's how the company will succeed, it's about the direction the CEO wants us to take." He knew he was showing some of his frustration, but how many times would he have to go over this? He was tired of explaining and explaining.

"I have a simple solution: you get the CEO to tell me to run my department by and for you." Willem doubted Eric would appreciate his effort to move toward conciliation, so he added, "We're not supposed to be dictated by your whim and fancy."

"Let's look at recent history." Eric tried not to be condescending, but he was both outraged and depressed that Willem was so stubborn when his department was supposed to be supporting sales.

"Your group was brought into the marketing division and changed from quality control to sales support to avoid these kinds of petty fights. You're supposed to be working with us."

"Agreed, but we were told to work with you, not for you." Willem also was intent on getting his point across, to teach Eric something. "It takes more than selling to a few customers to make a company like ours successful. We have to make sure we're selling the right product to the right people at the right time. The CEO said that, too."

"Bite your lip," Eric told himself as he felt the discussion slipping out of control. "I've got better things to do with my time than knock heads with a pig-headed Dutchman. Willem will get his due someday . . . he'll pay big for being out of touch." That thought helped change his tone and direction.

"Perhaps we don't have to decide our corporate vision today, and when we do we should invite the CEO and the VPs." Eric wanted to lighten the mood.

"Good idea." Willem smiled at Eric's joke because he, too, wanted to find a way out of the discussion. Yet Eric's teasing made him more suspicious. What kind of person would want to joke during a serious discussion? What were his motives? Somehow, Willem thought, Eric was not being honest.

Eric had given upon making any progress on how the departments could work together more effectively; their differences were too great to allow for a practical solution. But if he persisted a little more, he thought, he might be able to salvage something to bring back to his salespeople. "The real task at hand, and what prompted this visit, is that we need confirmation we can get that new system to DataLine at our negotiated price and time."

"Eric, you know your people aren't supposed to agree to such terms until they check with us. We can't have every salesperson setting prices and delivery dates around here. We have rules and procedures to protect prices and the company and to ensure we can properly support the product in our high-quality way."

Although he wanted to appease Willem and avoid another lecture, Eric couldn't stop saying, "My people felt they had to or lose the sale." He hoped Willem would take this as information.

"I don't see how it's good for us to try to be the low-cost source and always appear ready to lower our prices."

"Hey, it's a tough market out there, and we have to fight for market share." Eric tried to sound breezy. "Sometimes I wish the old days weren't gone, too."

"Haven't I heard this before?" Willem said.

"Let's get back to the issue. When can we have that confirmation?" Eric asked.

"I don't know."

"Can't you be a little more specific?" Eric thought he might have better luck with humor.

"I'll have to call a quick meeting with my people and then we'll decide. As you said, we're supposed to do things as a team now, and I've got to confer with my team."

"When might you be able to give us a yes or no?" Eric was determined to come away with something.

"The middle of next week, probably."

"Thanks . . . I think," Eric said, trying to smile.

"Don't mention it," Willem responded.

Eric felt he had gotten something for his team—the confirmation should be on the fast tract and they would know next week. But this discussion, as with most exchanges with Willem, had been wearing and taxing; he was glad he had already planned a long, hard run for the evening. His department would have to live with the uncertainty of the deal. He didn't like it, but felt he had no recourse but to let the customer assume the deal was approved. He didn't want to explain and complain to a customer about his own company.

The larger question was still unresolved. How could his group be expected to win contracts under such constraints? Certainly most of the smaller telecommunications companies did not operate with such impediments. Helix, where he worked before coming to NorTel, would have been dead in the water under such restraints.

He took some consolation from his belief that Willem and his group might be held accountable, though realistically that day was probably far off. Eric had not been with the company long enough to have the friends or the political skills required to get the VP to confront Willem's intransigence. The company was too old fashioned, too encrusted, and Willem had friends.

Lunch and a cold beer helped Eric regain his balance. Perhaps he had not done so badly in dealing with Willem after all. He hadn't blown his cool and told him off; that would have gotten him into trouble at conservative NorTel. He had showed discipline in defusing the situation and moving toward an answer to his problem. He could have done much worse.

He could also add this incident to his stories to help him convince his boss that his group faced unnecessary obstacles. He could more easily explain why even the modest growth in the sales figures was a very significant achievement for him and his group and thus confirm top management's decision to hire him away from Helix.

Eric wanted—though he could not fully admit it to himself—his group to recognize that he did well under the circumstances. His needs for reassurance were not lost on those who reported to him.

The reactions of Nick Slavik and Leslie Nielson, the salespeople who had negotiated the deal, did not surprise him. They were unhappy, but resigned to the Marketing Support Department's negative response.

"Those guys are so out of touch," Nick said.

"Someone should tell them they should try living in the twentieth century before the twenty-first," Leslie vented her frustration. "There must be something we can do with them."

"I've talked and I've talked, all I get back are clichés about rules and procedures," Eric said, with a mix of defiance and self-defense.

"Standards, standards, standards," Leslie mocked. "We can't eat standards."

"What can we realistically do? Eric can't go in there yelling and screaming." Nick wanted Eric to realize that he was not being blamed for failing to get a firm commitment.

"No, that just won't do at NorTel, that's for sure." Leslie followed Nick's lead.

"The VP already knows our problems, and we can't always whine to him," Nick said.

"You're right, there's not much Eric or the rest of us can do about the whole bureaucracy," Leslie said. She wanted to reassure Eric that she was not criticizing him for the delay in the confirmation.

Eric knew he could rely on his people. They were a team, fully committed to aggressive marketing and defending NorTel's market share. That support made fighting the cobwebs of the bureaucracy less exasperating. They knew they were on the right path.

Conflict's Lessons

Feeling trapped by their conflict, Eric and Willem tried to extradite themselves. They wanted the conflict to go away and to put their talents to work to find a way to get by. Although they knew the conflict was costly, they did not appreciate that they were missing important opportunities to become more competent and effective. Not only did they fail to reach an effective solution and serve the customer, they learned the wrong lessons. People always learn in conflict, but sometimes, like Eric and Willem, they reinforce stereotypes and biases, not develop more realistic, constructive views of conflict.

Conflict Is Inevitable

The conflict reinforced for Eric and Willem their misleading idea that conflict is an aberration. They continued to see conflict as an unwelcome stranger who disrupted their otherwise productive life. Many people are surprised that they must contend with conflict to get something done and have a relationship; their first impulse is to deny or avoid it. Conflict is not removed from our daily lives; it is very much at the heart of them. Conflict evolves from the nature of our relationships and situations as well as from our personalities.

During the heat of battle, Eric and Willem were so intent on blaming each other that they lost the perspective that their conflict was based on the way NorTel was organized and managed. The company oriented, selected, and trained the sales group to seek customers aggressively. Although a recent restructuring had changed it from the quality department to a marketing support group that reported to the marketing vice-president, Willem's group retained its directive to ensure that the company could deliver on contracts in a way that was both high-quality and profitable. With such mandates, it is unrealistic to expect harmony. Conflict is built into the departments' different agendas and the company's desire to have checks and balances.

NorTel's management style also made it more difficult for Eric and Willem to manage their conflict. Top management had assigned the departments complementary tasks that left them highly interdependent, but had not given the managers the tools and procedures to manage their conflicts constructively. Their common boss, the VP of marketing, would listen to each one complain about the other, but did little. He had similar ongoing battles with his peers at NorTel and assumed such clashes were an inevitable part of NorTel's way of doing business. To him, Willem and Eric got paid to take the heat and live with these conflicts.

The conflict also reflected the personalities and values of Eric and Willem. Eric was an action-oriented, practical sales manager with strong needs to be accepted and considered important. He wanted to fire up his team to market aggressively to customers, but his aggressiveness could grow into competitiveness as he dreamed of being a significant force at NorTel and of being given credit for turning the company's fortunes around. Such a reputation would also help him move quickly up the organization's ladder ahead of his peers and justify his struggles and sacrifices to succeed.

Willem wanted to be a highly competent professional whose integrity and knowledge commanded respect. He identified with quality assurance and was active in the field. He was firmly committed to doing the right thing, but in conflict this commitment easily transformed into intransigence. In his mind, he was prepared to be proven wrong, but this ideal was difficult for him to maintain in the heat of conflict. Accustomed to being direct and open about problems and conflicts, he had learned to be much more guarded and ambiguous since he had moved from The Netherlands to the United States five years before. He had assumed that Americans were, as they portrayed themselves, very direct. He soon paid the price for this assumption. He still bristled at how bosses, colleagues, and friends complained about his aggressive toughness and insensitivity.

Their personalities and situation made harmony completely unattainable. Yet Eric and Willem clung to the belief that they should be able to operate smoothly, without conflict. Their conflict did not help them re-examine this idea, but reinforced their thinking that conflict should be avoided. These sentiments resulted in disillusionment and unrealistic ways of coping.

Conflict Is Potentially Constructive

As a result of their interactions, Eric and Willem became more convinced that conflict is destructive. What they failed to appreciate is that their management of the conflict, not the conflict itself, got in their way.

Eric and his salespeople saw the conflict as preventing a quick, valid confirmation of the deal. Willem was confronted with evidence that he was not serving his "customers," the salespeople. Eric, Willem, and their employees spent time in meetings complaining about each other and coping with minor crises, not on important tasks with long-term payoffs. Their enduring conflict made it unlikely that they would get together formally or informally to develop more effective ways of marketing NorTel's products and services. They had to deal with crises, pick up the pieces, and try to get by.

In addition to these "bottom-line" consequences, the conflict undermined the mood and morale in the sales and support departments. Both managers felt unsupported and deprived of power. Eric and Willem had to deal with their strong feelings of anger and resentment without an opportunity to express them forcefully and directly. The conflict left them feeling unjustly put upon, waiting for revenge, and looking for a way to avoid future entanglements. They also needed to find an outlet for their stress. Eric had found running; too many people turn to abusing alcohol and drugs.

Instead of using the conflict as an opportunity to understand each other better, they reinforced stereotypes. Willem saw Eric's competitiveness, not his commitment to contributing to the company. Eric saw Willem's intransigence, not his professional knowledge and his desire to be open. They became less sensitive to the other as unique people and did not use the conflict to increase their self-awareness and feelings of being accepted and valued.

Yet, even their poorly managed conflict yielded some benefits. Eric and his group strengthened their image of themselves as innovators and breakers of the mold. By smashing the obstacles and encrusted bureaucracy, they would make NorTel successful in the increasingly competitive marketplace. Willem and his group reinforced their own self-image as a center of excellence dedicated to protecting the company from the excessive individualism of the sales force. The conflict provided a rallying and unifying cause for both the sales and the support group. Their mission, mixed with a sense of righteousness, was confirmed.

These gains were temporary and mixed. Their self-righteous views would lead to additional unproductive fights. The groups had to build their commitment to their vision and their cohesion on the firmer grounds of mutual cooperation and dedication to helping each other succeed.

If they had managed their conflict more effectively, Eric and Willem could have appreciated that conflict can be a highly constructive force in the lives of people and the success of organizations. When well-managed, conflict strengthens relationships and contributes to an organization's effectiveness. Dealing with conflict adds honesty and zest to relationships. People are confronted directly with the values, ideas, and perspectives of others and are invited to know them as distinct persons. They attend to and respond to each other's requests and needs; feeling valued by others, they value and accept themselves more.

Conflict is the medium by which problems are recognized and solved. People who discuss conflict disclose information, challenge assumptions, dig into issues, and, as a consequence, understand problems thoroughly and make successful decisions. Conflict is needed because diverse opinions and information are mandatory to solve problems and get things done.

Productive conflict in organizations improves quality, reduces costs, upgrades leadership, stimulates brainstorming and teamwork, and institutes new procedures to improve company operations. Conflict is not the problem; conflict is part of the solution.

Conflict Must Be Addressed

Eric and Willem were not learning the value of open, skillful discussion of conflict; instead, they were hoping that somehow they could avoid emotional exchanges in the future. They failed to realize that the conflict was harmful because they were expending much more energy on avoiding and smoothing over their differences than talking about them directly. The two groups gossiped and complained about each other, but very seldom even talked to each other. They ate in different parts of the lunchroom, frequented different bars, and celebrated holidays separately. At the company picnic, they quickly and nervously greeted each other and then settled into the more relaxing, easy camaraderie of their own group.

Even when a crisis pushed Eric and Willem to talk directly, they avoided underlying issues. They hinted at but only ambiguously revealed their mistrust and lack of confidence in each other. Rather than leading to an open discussion, these hints were considered innuendos and insults. They used humor to move away from hot issues. They concluded that the only practical approach was to fall back on a narrowly defined task they could make some headway on. The divide between them deepened.

Conflict with Cooperation

Poorly managed conflict can easily mislead protagonists into adopting distorted, ineffective ways of viewing and defining conflict. Eric and Willem misunderstood their conflict to mean that they were against each other. They were working at cross-purposes; their goals were opposing goals and their perspectives were irreconcilable.

Conflict is foremost a sign of interdependence, not necessarily of competitive, incompatible goals. People with cooperative interests are often in conflict as they express their opposing views about the best way to complete common tasks, divide up their work, demonstrate respect and affection, and distribute the benefits of their collaborative effort.

Although not all their goals were compatible, Eric and Willem were largely cooperatively interdependent. Developing long-term customers by providing high-quality service, becoming a highly respected marketing division with clout in the company, and maintaining the profitability of the firm depended upon their successful collaboration. Their own status and job security also depended upon furthering these common interests.

Their poor conflict management fed their competitiveness and emphasized their opposing mandates, their efforts to appear more important to their boss, and their attempts to be right and have the other wrong. Incidents of effective collaboration were lost in the fires of their battles. They were losing sight of the reality that they could only attain long-term success if both were effective.

Cooperation and conflict are not opposites; our choice is not between working together and conflict. Our studies indicate that people in competition find the most reasons to try to avoid conflict. They expect that others will ridicule and ignore their demands and may use what they say against them. People in cooperation have the confidence that others will respond open-mindedly to their requests.

The Need to Develop Conflict Skills

One of the most enduring and misleading of all popular attitudes toward conflict is that people avoid conflict or handle it aggressively because they want to. Eric and Willem blamed the conflict on the ill-will of the other. Their conclusion that the other was purposely getting in their way fueled their anger. It was redoubled when they remembered that the other was supposed to be on the same company "team."

But motivation to managing conflict well is not enough and is often not a major obstacle. Both Eric and Willem wanted to have effective work relationships and to avoid heated, unproductive exchanges. Indeed, they were too motivated in that they wanted a quick fix that would restore harmony.

Most people want open relationships in which issues are discussed honestly and sensitively. However, their fears and misconceptions about conflict get in their way. They doubt they have the communication, emotional, and intellectual abilities to meet the demands of conflict management; they doubt that others are motivated and able to manage conflict.

Eric and Willem had some conflict skills. They kept a lid on the conflict and avoided abusive insults, made some progress on their task, and kept some collaboration going. Yet these skills may not have been as useful as they thought. Explosive conflict could have made it obvious to Eric, Willem, and their boss that the status quo was intolerable and that they would have to discuss their relationship thoroughly and make changes.

We learn much from conflict. If handled cooperatively, we learn valuable lessons about ourselves, our partners, and how to solve problems and feel confident and powerful. But, if mishandled, we can reinforce misleading stereotypes and lower our views of ourselves and our conflict partners.

To learn requires valid ideas to analyze our conflicts and the ability to get a realistic perspective on them. Here, too, Eric and Willem lost in their conflict because they felt unable and unprepared to discuss and reflect on their conflict together. They were stuck in their own views and framework and, thus, were destined to repeat their ineffective battles. They were learning the wrong lessons and, tragically, undermining their ability to learn with each other.

Learning from Conflict

Guides for Action

- Recognize the inevitability of conflict.
- Appreciate the potential value of conflict.
- Understand that conflict changes attitudes and skills.
- Recognize that learning to manage conflict is an investment in relationships and productivity.
- Use present conflicts to develop abilities.
- Learn with conflict partners.
- Use conflicts to empower yourself and others.
- Apply the cooperative conflict idea to your conflicts.
- Learn from small as well as large conflicts.
- Learn from successes as well as failures.
- Use conflict to manage change.

Pitfalls to Avoid

- Assume that attitudes and ideas about conflict are fixed.
- Dismiss learning as only for young people.
- Believe you have had so many conflicts that you cannot learn more.
- Assume learning and action, ideas and practice are unconnected.
- Believe that the solution to your conflicts is for others to be kinder.
- Seek techniques that will give you a negotiating edge over your partners.
- Wait for traumatic events and crises to learn.
- Concentrate on short-term task completion and always postpone learning.
- Neglect reflecting and learning from experiences.
- Blame conflicts on the other person.
- Blame conflicts on yourself.
- Let conflict and change control you.

3

Using Conflict to Learn to Manage Conflict

The person who grabs the cat by the tail learns about 44 percent faster than the one just watching.

—Mark Twain

"What a damn pain," Eric swore to himself. "So many things to do and a stubborn Dutchman, too." After talking with Nick and Leslie, he had finally gotten back to his unending list of tasks and meetings. It felt good to be busy again. Now, as he was driving home, his attention returned to his fight. He felt as he had when, as a salesman, he had lost a big sale. He was dejected but determined not to let it get him down.

He was relieved that he could be free of serious conflict at home. Although he and his wife, Carol, had had many arguments, they gradually had accommodated each other. He knew her hot spots—namely, how messy the house was and her weight gain. He had learned to avoid those issues, though he could not completely reconcile himself to them. He had been brought up to think that there are two kinds of people, those who keep their houses clean and those who do not. She had gained a pound for the each of the nine years they were married, and the weight meant that, while still pretty, she was no longer beautiful. He felt he was being realistic. He knew of few marriages totally free of disappointments and deceits.

He knew his wife liked a drink with dinner, and he had worked out a way to join her by taking a small one and eating a light meal. That way he would not feel bloated when he ran later that night. He was both amused and annoyed during the meal by Alexandria, his daughter, and Ron, his son, who were their usual noisy, rambunctious selves.

He mentioned his fight to Carol, who listened dutifully and agreed that Willem was unreasonable and mean-spirited. But she did not respond as compassionately and emotionally to his troubles as she did when they were first married. Perhaps, he thought, she had grown tired of hearing about work problems or thought it was unnecessary now that he was a fast track manager and no longer on commissions.

The highlight of his day was just ahead as he drove to the gym. He would laugh and talk with his friend of twenty years, Anthony, and take a exhausting, exhilarating run. He would feel cleansed and relieved afterward.

"You seem even more distracted than usual tonight," Anthony said, after they had run the first half mile. "Been fighting with Carol?"

Eric was surprised by Anthony's comment because he thought he had joked with Anthony as usual while they were getting ready to run. He was not offended, however, because Anthony was an old friend.

"No, that Willem guy from so-called marketing support is on my back. It's my bad luck to have to work with a pig-headed Dutchman." Remembering that Anthony was of Dutch ancestry, Eric added, "I hope you don't mind the literary allusion."

"I know some stubborn Dutchmen myself, and some stubborn Swedes, some stubborn Chinese. . . . I've seen many," Anthony said. He had traveled a great deal as a college student, spent two years in the Peace Corps in the back hills of the Philippines, and had taken assorted jobs in the Far East and Europe. Finally, he had returned to his home town to settle down.

Eric told him about the latest incident. "So do you feel sorry for me?"

"Sure. The price of success in corporate America can be steep indeed," Anthony said, with his natural mix of humor and candor, sarcasm and sympathy. "Let me tell you the costs of having to begin at the bottom of the ladder at age thirty-five." Anthony felt he had paid a price for his international adventures, but he knew it was not in him to do what Eric had done.

"Yes, corporate success can be a problem," Eric responded to the candor, but not the humor, in Anthony's comment.

Anthony turned serious, too. He had been contemplating Eric's conflicts with Willem and others at NorTel and trying to formulate his thoughts into words. "You don't want to put up with the fighting any more, right?"

"You got it."

"Then don't."

"Good idea! I can see you as a no-nonsense management consultant."

"Level with him, tell him you're fed up with how things have been going and that you want changes."

"Right. We can't get him to agree to give us a fast confirmation; now you want me to insist and force him to do things differently."

"I said level *with* him, not level him." Anthony knew that humor helped Eric think about sensitive issues. "He's probably complaining about the situation right now, just like you are."

"Anthony, if he wanted to end the conflict, he would have done so long ago. He thinks he can satisfy his ego if he can protect the purity and strength of his group. He's not interested in doing something about the conflict, other than fighting and making my life miserable."

"So he's sadistic and dumb, and he beats up his wife."

"Of course not. Some people even like him, but they aren't fighting him."

"Exactly. And you don't want to be, either; but you can't just wish things would be different, you have to do something about it."

"Why should I take the first step and the risks? He's the one being so stubborn."

"One thing I've learned about people, including Dutch people, is that while you might think they are unreasonable, stubborn, and crazy, when you understand where they're coming from, they seldom are."

They both wanted to move away from serious talk. They began comparing how their bodies were holding up under the fast pace and commenting on how some of the female runners resembled the women they had known and dated in high school and university. As they drew near the end of their five miles, they grew quiet and quickened their pace. As Anthony pulled away, Eric resigned himself to falling behind again.

After showering and settling in at the gym bar, Anthony said, "I won the race so I buy the beers." Actually, as Anthony always won, they changed the rules so that they would alternate buying.

"After your idea about leveling with Willem, I think you should buy me two beers. Your idea is from the back country of the Philippines."

"Hey, you should see the people I worked with there. If they had a problem, they'd go right for it. Arguing, debating, and agreeing. We should be so good."

"But I'm arguing with a modern American type, and a Dutch one at that."

"Those Dutch are good, too. They like to debate issues."

"That's right, you really liked it there." Eric was beginning to see that Anthony's idea was worth considering. He liked the directness of the approach and it seemed to offer a possible way out. He had had enough of patience and lip biting. "You never know, Willem may be glad to talk about it, too. Stranger things have happened."

"I think he might and, if he doesn't, what's the risk?"

"Just that we'll never get a confirmation again."

"In which case, he'll be history and your problem will be solved."

"I'll have to think about it."

"Do. Run on Friday?"

"Be prepared to lose."

Driving home, Eric felt relaxed and energized from the run and from talking to Anthony. It was almost as if the conflict with Willem was not so large. It struck him as strange that he had to struggle to see his conflict with Willem in the way Anthony found so easy. When he awoke the next morning, he knew he had a challenge ahead of him.

Using Conflict to Manage Conflict

Eric was getting what he wanted from Carol, Nick, and Leslie. They listened to his concerns, allowed him to vent his feelings, and reassured him that they were on his side. After the fight with Willem frustrated his goals and disrupted his image of himself as competent and respected, Eric needed to hear that they were with him. Yet it took a conflict with Anthony to give him a more useful approach to managing his conflict with Willem.

His wife and employees recognized Eric's need for confirmation very clearly, in part because they also wanted to be seen as worthwhile, effective people after a rocky fight. Nick and Leslie saw themselves as loyal employees who supported their boss. They were team players who defended their group from the abuse of the support department. The idea of bucking Eric when he was down seemed noxious as well as dangerous to their careers.

Early in their marriage, Carol had developed the practice of listening to her husband's successes and frustrations. She wanted to be a loyal, loving wife and share in the drama of the workplace. But her motivation and practice had changed over the years. In part because of her growing frustration with what she considered her limited world, she had become less patient with just listening and agreeing. She began to point out what she saw as Eric's repeated errors of judgment. Unfortunately, Eric responded only to the frustration behind her remarks, not to the validity of her arguments. To keep the peace, she now restricted herself to listening and agreeing, though it was more difficult to be patient.

Anthony, too, saw himself as a faithful friend who wanted to show he was on Eric's side. But he differed from Carol, Nick, and Leslie in that he saw challenging Eric's thinking as a viable way to demonstrate his loyalty. Although he did not use these terms, he grasped the potential of cooperative, constructive conflict. He could disagree with Eric and still be on the same side. Indeed, the conflict was used to promote Eric's feelings of competence and well-being and to reaffirm Anthony's friendship.

One reason for Anthony's insight into the value of challenging Eric was that, as an outsider, he brought a fresh perspective to the conflict at NorTel. His experiences of living and working in other countries had made him flexible in his thinking and actions. He compared how he was taught to handle problems and conflicts with those he had experienced in other countries. He had fewer illusions about how openly and effectively American organizations manage conflict. He was highly skeptical of Eric's labeling of Willem as a stubborn Dutchman.

Anthony was confident that he could confront Eric successfully.

Carol, Nick, and Leslie suppressed their doubts about Eric's effectiveness because they did not believe they could act on them. Anthony had been Eric's firm friend for over twenty years, and their friendship had survived the trials of high school and university, fights over dating partners, and long separations. Anthony was not implicated in office politics, nor was he a rival for promotions. Twenty years of teasing and talking had given him the savvy to get his point across without insulting Eric. Eric would see Anthony's good intentions, not dismiss them as mean-spirited, and would consider his views open-mindedly.

Eric was more open to Anthony's message than it appeared to his wife and employees. Eric saw himself as a hands-on, supportive manager who dealt directly and honestly with people. He found that Anthony's suggestion fitted his action-orientation style. He wanted to do something, and a direct discussion on how they were managing their conflict might be the answer.

Managing Conflict Together

Eric was highly motivated to have an open relationship with Willem. He not only wanted quicker, easier approvals and schedules, but also an end to the haranguing. However, wanting, by itself, was not enough to bring about success. Through his conflict with Anthony, he began to outline a realistic way to achieve these aspirations and to feel the energy and direction needed to confront the conflict. He was learning that he could not resolve the conflict by imposition; he had to work with Willem to manage it.

Anthony helped Eric understand that blaming Willem as a person was ultimately counterproductive. Seeing himself as right and blameless helped Eric maintain a self-image of competence; holding Willem responsible and labeling him as stubborn gave him the temporary pleasure of feeling superior. But these attitudes also led Eric to argue that Willem should change and accept his solutions to problems, actions that fueled the painful conflict and blocked ways out of it.

Eric found it difficult to accept that he was part of the problem and that he, too, needed to change. After all, he knew his intentions were honest and well-meaning. But he was coming to appreciate that Willem might have had good intentions as well.

Anthony was a very credible adviser who Eric could not easily dismiss. Anthony's method reinforced his message and showed Eric how conflict could be addressed. Anthony wanted Eric to level with Willem as he was leveling with Eric. Eric was reminded that he and Willem did not have to support each other by agreeing. Anthony was direct and helped Eric form his own opinions; Anthony did not try to force or impose his conclusions. Conflict can be positive if people work together to manage it.

By reminding Eric that he should be honest and deal with issues openly and constructively, Anthony had resurrected an important, straightforward message that had gotten lost in the dynamics of the battle. But just telling Eric to be more open was not enough. Eric also needed a sense of how he could put these values into action and believe he could do it. Through his conflict with Anthony, Eric began to formulate a direction for how to approach Willem more effectively.

Eric was beginning to appreciate that if he wanted to feel powerful, then Willem would also have to feel powerful; if he wanted to manage conflict, then Willem would have to be able to manage conflict. The next chapter describes cooperative conflict in which people manage their conflicts for mutual benefit.

Discuss Conflict Handling with Supporters

Guides for Action

- Appreciate that ineffective conflict frustrates learning as well as getting things done.
- Develop open relationships in which you can get feedback on how you handle your conflicts.
- Consider alternative approaches to managing conflict.

Pitfalls to Avoid

- Seek confirmation that you are right and your protagonist is wrong.
- Appear too strong and confident to be challenged.
- Appear too weak and fragile to be challenged.
- Use gossip to discredit your protagonist's.
- Demonstrate your competence by being stubborn and intransigent.

PART TWO

Laying the Foundations
for Learning

*Yet I am sure that a consideration of general purposes, "principles,"
and underlying conceptions—what we may call the philosophical approach to concrete problems—is intensely practical. Indeed, it is almost
necessary that we unite in such an approach in order that our consideration of the specific problems may be intelligent, and our discussion of
them may be intelligible.*

—*Chester Barnard*
Management theorist, 1935

Theory, experience, and relationships are the major ingredients of learning
to manage conflict. As people discuss conflict ideas and reflect on their
conflicts, they gain a sharper picture of the nature of cooperative conflict,
develop better insight into their own approaches, and appreciate more
clearly their strengths and characteristics that need improvement. They
can then decide how to make their conflicts more productive. Chapter 4
describes cooperative conflict theory and reviews its research base.
Chapter 5 shows how people can work together to learn about cooperative
conflict and apply it to their own conflicts. Chapter 6 indicates how to use
cooperative conflict to build a network of people committed to learning.

4

Cooperative Conflict Theory

Victory is by nature insolent and haughty.
—Cicero

"Why does it seem so complicated now, when last night it seemed straightforward?" Eric said to himself on the way to work. "I have lots to do today . . . maybe I should postpone talking to Willem until tomorrow." But that thought did not sit well, either. "I'll be busy tomorrow, too, and if I don't do it today, Anthony will razz me about being a coward. Besides, Anthony's right. I don't want to live with this conflict." Eric worried about how to approach Willem but had no concrete plan by the time he reached his office.

Halfway through the morning, he saw Leslie in Nick's office and was drawn to say hello. With a moment's hesitation, he began. "Team, I got an idea."

"'Teamwork and ideas—dynamite combination," Nick joked.

"Please don't say dynamite," Eric smiled. "This is about how we can defuse our conflict with Willem, not explode it."

"Wouldn't dynamite in their office do that?" Leslie deadpanned. "We wouldn't light it, of course; just let them whiff the consequences if we did."

"That's consistent with the NorTel culture," Nick said. "We fight dirty, but quietly."

"My idea is to tell Willem that we're tired of fighting and ask him to work with us to find a way we can work together better." Eric was pleased with how neatly that came out. Perhaps he had learned what Anthony was talking about. "Any reactions?"

"My assessment: risky, aggressive—a salesperson's thing to do, but not a NorTel sort of thing," Nick said.

"We always have to take risks with our customers, but it seems riskier with Willem," Leslie said. "If a customer tells us to get lost, we find another. But if he tells you that, what do we do then?"

"Yes, that would be a problem. . ." Eric felt perplexed again.

"Then we could feel very self-righteous," Nick said. "We'll tell the world what a turkey he is."

"It could be that he wants to put an end to all this bickering too," Eric offered.

"A possibility," Leslie said.

"He doesn't appear to want to end the fight," Nick said. "But you could put him on the spot and find out if he wants to continue the bickering. If he says yes, he'll look like a fool."

"Interesting idea," Eric said. "It would be great if he said he wanted to stop fighting, but I think we can't give him the impression that we're trying to trick or force him. Those tactics backfire with Willem."

Eric felt invigorated as he went back to his office. Then he remembered that it would be much more stressful talking to Willem than to Nick and Leslie. He couldn't back away now because his team expected him to proceed.

"So simple, yet so complicated at the same time," Eric muttered to himself. As a salesman, taking with people and taking risks were natural, everyday tasks. Leslie was right; the risk was larger and the task harder with Willem.

He knew that the meeting should be face-to-face and natural. Telephoning or calling a meeting seemed too impersonal and formal. He would drop in on Willem as he did with Nick and Leslie. He wanted to keep the discussion relaxed and upbeat. Getting angry and tough with Willem never worked.

Although he could envisage himself asking Willem if he wanted to end the fighting, he could not feel comfortably in charge. He had no contingency plans as he did when making a pitch to a customer. He would have to plunge in and stay quick on his feet, calling upon all his skills to stay cool and keep the discussion under control.

"Good afternoon," Eric tried to be cheerful. Wondering whether he sounded too cheerful made him slow to respond to Willem's greeting. "Stay with it," he told himself. "You can't turn back now."

"What I came to talk about is our problem working together." Eric had planned some small talk first, but, feeling awkward and seeing the perhaps suspicious, perhaps just puzzled look on Willem's face, he decided to plunge in.

"Yes . . . problems," Willem said guardedly. "What new crisis do you have for me today?"

"No crisis," Eric said, reminding himself that he did not want to get angry with Willem. "I thought that a good talk about how we're working together would clear the air and help us have fewer crises." Eric felt reassured; perhaps the prior discussions had prepared him after all.

"Nice-sounding sentiments . . . something one could expect from a salesman." Though in fact he welcomed Eric's serious overture, Willem's anger welled up and felt very real. "What do you propose exactly?"

"I thought we could talk person-to-person and agree that we should find a better way of collaborating. I don't enjoy the present way, and I don't think you do, either."

"Enjoy? I thought you guys were too interested in sales and commissions for that."

"We know how to have a good time. You know those fancy restaurants and elaborate entertainments we have to go to in the line of duty." Eric hoped that self-depreciating humor would help.

But Willem got angrier and looked coldly into Eric's eyes. "You come in unannounced to tell me that we must now do things differently, talk in generalities, and now you want to joke about it all. I don't like that." His excessive frustration and anger sought ventilation.

"Be patient," Eric told himself. "Don't those customer service manuals call this a moment of truth, where things could go either way?" That reminder helped, but he still couldn't avoid sounding annoyed as he spoke, "I'm trying to deal with this issue honestly and directly. I may not be doing such a good job, but I'm trying."

Seeing Eric's growing irritation, Willem knew that he would have to control his anger and show that he, too, wanted to find a way out. Yet he was hesitant to be too open; he had done that too often with Eric and other Americans. "What are you proposing exactly?"

"I thought that you might be as tired of us fighting against each other as I am and that we should find a better way of working together."

"There's a logic there. But I have been trying, trying very hard," Willem said.

"But we haven't tried together. Instead, you've tried your way and I've tried mine."

"I'll have to think about that one." The tension was leaving Willem's voice and he cracked a smile. "Have you been listening to a new motivation tape by the latest marketing guru?"

"Maybe I should be doing some reading."

"There are lots of things to read." Willem wanted to take a break from discussing how they dealt with their conflicts. "You should see this new book on new product teams I've been reading."

"Sounds interesting; there are exciting developments about teamwork in business these days." But Eric wanted to press on with the issue at hand. "I've been talking with salespeople about finding a new way of working with marketing support."

"It's easy to say that our discussions should be better."

"We don't always fight against each other." Eric paused. "I think we should see if we can get better."

"What would this new way look like? I can't see us living in perfect harmony, we're too different for that."

"We would find a better way of discussing our differences. Without rancor and with compromise."

"Win–win negotiating, isn't that what they call it? We work things out to find solutions that are good for both of us. I've always been willing to try. How is the problem."

They talked more about how they might proceed. They agreed on generalities: they should be honest, courteous, respectful and helpful, but they did not have a road map for how to put these generalities into place when they clearly had past and present conflicts. They decided to read some materials on how they could work together more effectively and deal with their conflicts.

Eric sought out Nick and Leslie to tell them that the meeting went well and that Willem wanted to find a better approach. He was relieved, but he did not want to disclose that he also felt bruised. Willem's cold eyes, sarcasm, and hard tone bothered Eric more than he wanted to admit.

The next evening Eric drove to the gym for his workout with Anthony. He was feeling better about the conflict and was eager to tell Anthony the good news.

"Well, I did it," Eric announced as they changed.

"Whatever you did, I'm happy for you," Anthony laughed.

"I talked to Willem about the conflict, and I think I leveled with him without leveling him."

"I was meaning to ask about that. Was he as stubborn as you thought?"

"He said he's been trying to find a better way, and I told him I was, too, but we have agreed to find that better way together."

"Big step, I bet you feel relieved and proud."

"I feel much less burdened; I'm not sure about proud."

"Why not? You took the first steps to turn things around. Heroic stuff."

"We're not talking great literature here, just trying to make things a little better," Eric said.

"Perhaps you're right. But you should feel good about it."

"I felt beaten up afterwards. He wasn't all peaches and cream."

"That's natural. He's probably got a lot of frustration and anger that he wanted to get rid of. I bet you surprised him. After all, he hasn't been thinking about how to resolve the conflict the last two days, as you have."

"I guess he did seem caught off guard," Eric reflected.

"Sounds like you kept your cool. Twenty years of selling experience pays off."

"I needed all of it."

"You can't expect to change the relationship instantly. It took time to deteriorate; it will take time to build up. What does your group think of all this?"

"They seemed pleased Willem and I made progress."

"That's important, Eric. You want your team with you on this one."

"Do you have any suggestions about how we could proceed?"

Anthony looked puzzled. "Keep talking, I guess. Keep the momentum up and the lines of communication open."

"We need some reading about working out differences and managing conflict. Do you have recommendations?"

"You could do worse than *War and Peace* followed by *Fathers and Sons*. Modern writers like Taylor and Dubus are terrific on the dilemmas of husbands and wives."

"Once an English major, always an English major. We were thinking of something a little more focused on our particular problem. Our human resources manager gave me some leads."

"The two of you are going to read together?"

"We both need to learn how to do this better . . . to get on the same wavelength to manage our conflicts."

"Could be fun following this adventure."

"You won't have so much fun losing the run. Tonight is my night."

Cooperative Discussion of Conflict Management

Eric and Willem had come to appreciate that an open discussion focused directly on how they were managing their conflicts would be vital to breaking free of grudges and bickering. Discussing how they could improve their conflict management together could be a powerful approach to learning to work together more productively.

Typically, people in conflict focus their discussions on the issues and tasks at hand. They elaborate their positions and refute the arguments of their opponents. Yet people are very much concerned about how they are managing their conflicts and their relationships. When conflicts are well managed, they feel good about their discussions and relationships and see each other as honest and open-minded. When the conflict is poorly managed, people blame their conflict partners and consider them stubborn, dishonest, arrogant, and closed-minded. If the conflict gets hot, they may voice their criticisms and complaints. This blaming raises the stakes and makes it a "personal conflict." When people feel their personal competence has been questioned, they counterattack and become more intransigent, reactions that escalate the conflict and paralyze progress.

Eric and Willem were determined to move away from blaming each other toward helping each other become more effective and able to deal with their conflicts. They were coming to understand that they had a common interest in each other's learning. They would be more successful at managing conflict and leading their groups if both of them were more skilled.

How they would achieve this mutual learning was similar to what they would learn. They were going to learn to manage their conflicts cooperatively and productively through cooperative work and discussions of how they handled their conflicts. To do this effectively, Eric and Willem needed a crisp understanding of cooperation and its alternatives.

Getting Your Antagonist to Talk and Deal

Eric took the first steps toward opening a discussion with Willem about his frustrations in handling their conflicts and the possibility of together forging a new way. Willem eventually welcomed Eric's invitation, in part because he, like Eric, recognized that they would work more effectively if they got along better.

Sometimes antagonists have stopped talking altogether and would rebuke any attempt to open a dialogue on anything—much less on improving how they manage conflict. The other is at fault, and the other should change and suffer. It is one of life's great tragedies that people, groups, and countries can remain mired in this painful stalemate for years, even decades.

Ultimately, Eric was dependent on Willem. Eric could not effectively manage the conflict by himself; conflict management is much easier when both persons are learning together. But often we feel that the most difficult and problematic step toward conflict management is the first one: opening up discussion and getting the other committed to talking. We see the other as closed and unreflective by nature, or perhaps as mean and sadistic or even committed to treating us in a cruel, exploitative way. What can be done?

There are no sure-fire strategies. Ultimately, your conflict partners will make their own choices about how they will deal with the conflict; unfortunately, they may chose stonewalling and the status quo. There are several points to consider when you develop a way to approach your antagonist to begin a discussion of improving conflict management.

Do not, as Eric did, overestimate your antagonist's intransigence. We often project our fears onto opponents and blame the conflict on their lack of caring and sensitivity. They, in turn, blame the conflict on our insensitivity. A CEO realized that his two most important managers were discussing their conflicts through him. He was frustrated because he had to spend so much time listening and explaining their positions to each other. He assumed that their harsh, set attitudes toward each other would make it difficult for them to confront their ineffective ways of handling conflict. After weeks of hesitating, he distributed readings on cooperative conflict and prepared himself for a tough, emotional day of bargaining. Much to his surprise, they quickly agreed that they had been foolish and got down to the business of developing more useful procedures.

Asking your opponent to discuss and improve how you both are handling conflict may get you a no, but you should also try to understand more clearly the strength of this intransigence and the reasons for it. Such knowledge can help you better understand and deal with the conflict. You should also be prepared, as Eric was, to be credible and to give your opponent consistent cues that you want an open, mutual discussion. The idea of talking about conflict may seem strange to your opponent or may even be interpreted as your ploy to get the upper hand. Your antagonist may want clear evidence that you are committed to finding mutually beneficial ways of dealing with conflict.

You and your antagonist can both confront the tangible and psychological costs of the poorly managed conflict and appreciate the value of productive conflict. Often people rationalize these costs by believing that the other is—or soon will be—losing more than they are and discounting the benefits of productive conflict. ("I'm tough, I can take it at least as long as he can." "She'll pay for this." "We would never be able to get along.")

How to discuss the issue of costs and benefits depends on the situation. Your options include: (1) disclosing your frustrations, losses, and hopes and asking your antagonist to reciprocate; (2) brainstorming and debating together how productive conflict could be useful; and (3) challenging your opponent's defense that he or she suffers little. Confronting the costs and benefits should be cooperative. You want to convey that you are not gloating over your opponent's losses or laughing at his or her irrationality and that you are suffering real losses that you could but do not want to bear.

Try to signal that the conflict can be constructively resolved. Avoid blaming, affronting face, and in other ways making the other person defensive and closed-minded. Be hard on the problem, but soft on the person. To make dealing with the conflict more acceptable, demonstrate that you are trying to understand the other person's perspective and acting inconsistently with your opponent's negative stereotypes of you.

Empower your antagonist. Show that you are open to negotiation and are flexible about the final outcome of conflict. Indicate that you believe there might be better solutions than the ones you are now proposing. Suggest options and ask your opponent to choose the best one.

Appreciating that there are alternatives to a negotiated settlement can help manage conflict. In many circumstances, we can withdraw from the relationship at some time. We may have to put up with a boss who is a bully, but bosses do not last forever. High rates of divorce, job switching, and high geographical mobility all suggest that finding an alternative is a popular, though often unwisely used, approach to conflict management. Finding an alternative can be overused—a wife runs away before checking her assumptions that her marriage can't be improved— and it can be underused—a repeatedly abused wife stays. Even when we cannot withdraw physically, we can usually withdraw psychologically and change our thinking. Chapter 9 considers how to ventilate and change our thinking so that we are less angry and depressed about conflict.

Your antagonist may refuse to talk and deal, despite your persistent efforts. Although you may experience a painful rejection, you can congratulate yourself on having the courage to try. After your antagonist has clearly indicated an unwillingness to negotiate, you can feel assured that you now have solid reasons for concluding that he or she will not try to repair the relationship and improve how conflicts are handled. You can also appreciate the costs of intransigence and know you are not prepared to make such a costly mistake.

Cooperation and Competition

Morton Deutsch, a pioneer in social psychology since the 1940s, argued that discovering how people believe their goals are related is a useful way to understand how they work together. He proposed that whether people believe their goals are predominantly cooperative or competitive affects their expectations and actions and, thereby, the consequences of conflict. Hundreds of studies have developed this theory and shown it to be an elegant, powerful way to understand conflict.

The Alternatives

In cooperation, people believe their goals are positively related, so that as one moves toward goal attainment, others move toward their goals. They understand that as one succeeds, others succeed. People in cooperation want each other to pursue their goals effectively, for the other's effectiveness helps all of them reach their goals. If one swims, the others swim; if one sinks, the others sink. They feel like a team working on the same side.

Their individual achievement depends upon the achievements of others. Cooperation is not based on altruism, but on the recognition that, with positively related goals, self-interests require collaboration. For example, cooperative members of a new product team want each other to develop useful ideas and work hard to create a new product that makes everyone successful. Cooperative work integrates self-interest to achieve mutual goals.

Alternatively, people may believe their goals are competitive in that one's goal attainment precludes or at least makes less likely the goal attainment of others. If one succeeds, others must fail. If one wins, others lose. People in competition conclude that they are better off when others act ineffectively; when others are productive, they are less likely to succeed themselves. A competitive team member wants to prove that he is the most capable and that his ideas are superior; he is frustrated when others develop useful ideas and work hard. Competitive work pits individuals against each other in a fight to win.

Whether people conclude that their goals are primarily cooperative or competitive, Deutsch theorized, profoundly affects people's orientation and intentions toward each other. In cooperation, people want others to act effectively and expect others to want them to be effective because it is in each person's self-interest to do so. They trust that their risks and efforts will be welcomed and reciprocated. They believe they can rely upon each other and are sensitive and responsive to each other.

These positive expectations lead to discussions that integrate and combine perspectives and interests. Studies document that people in cooperation share information, see each other's points of view, communicate and influence effectively, exchange resources, assist and support each other, discuss opposing ideas openly, and use higher-quality reasoning. These actions, in turn, help cooperators move forward by completing tasks, agreeing to high-quality solutions, reducing stress, liking each other, and strengthening work relationships and confidence in future collaboration.

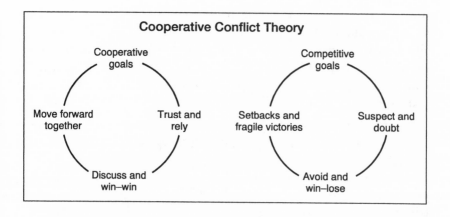

Cooperative goals help people manage their conflicts productively. They recognize that it is in everyone's self-interest to promote each other's effectiveness. Feeling trusting, they freely speak their minds, reveal their frustrations, and talk about their anger. Antagonists welcome confrontations and realize that it is important to work out settlements so that they can continue to assist each other. They work for win–win solutions that maintain and strengthen the relationship. They explore each other's perspectives, creatively integrate their views, and are confident they will continue to work together for mutual benefit. As a result, they are prepared to discuss future conflicts.

Competitive goals, on the other hand, create the suspicion that people will promote their own interests at others' expense and interfere with each other. Their mistrust restricts the exchange of information and resources and distorts communication; people often try to avoid direct discussions and, when compelled to discuss, try to impose their positions and to avoid losing. This avoidance alternating with escalating conflict frustrates productivity, intensifies stress, and lowers morale.

Competitive goals make managing conflict very difficult and can lead to debilitating fights. With competitive goals, people suspect that self-interests will lead to mutual frustration. They doubt others are interested in their feelings and frustrations, and they fear ridicule. Although they often prefer to avoid conflict—especially with their bosses and others with authority and power who can "win" and impose their wishes—the underlying problems continue to frustrate. If they do confront their antagonist, they often do so in a tough, dominating manner that escalates the conflict. Whether they choose to avoid or confront conflict, competitors, although they may believe they have won in the short term, usually end up feeling that they have lost and only hope that others have lost more.

Organizational Conflict

Traditionally, an effective organization is thought to be a well-run machine, free of conflict. But it is well-managed conflict that contributes substantially to organizational success. Recent studies document specifically that cooperative conflict gets ordinary and extraordinary tasks done for organizations.

Conflict management, for example, is essential for successful innovation. The demands of the marketplace and workplace require organizations to innovate and adapt, to become "learning organizations." They are experimenting with new procedures and management styles and developing new products and services to respond to technological advances, competition, and consumer preferences.

Faculty members and employees of a large postsecondary educational institution were interviewed on occasions when they were able to solve problems in new and creative ways and in instances when they were unable to develop a new approach. When they discussed their opposing views openly and forthrightly and considered all views, they were able to develop innovative solutions. When they discussed issues from only one point of view and were unable to incorporate different views, they failed to make progress and developed solutions that lacked quality and creativity.

Managers have long complained that employees resist new technological innovations and, as a consequence, investments in technology do not pay off in the expected productivity increases. Less recognized is that employees must identify problems and discuss solutions to use the technology. A retail chain's employees who had cooperative goals were able to use new scanning technology more efficiently because they exchanged information and hammered out ideas about how to solve the many problems the technology had created.

Managers are restructuring and transforming organizations.

They are cutting management levels, splitting up businesses, forming links across business units, and using task teams and parallel structures to create synergy. However, restructuring seldom results in the expected improvements in the quality of products, productivity, and work life for employees or in greater returns for shareholders. A large telecommunications high technology firm had undergone waves of restructuring, but without noticeable improvement. Interviews revealed that changing structures was insufficient. Employees had to make use of any new structure, and to do this they had to coordinate and manage their conflicts. When they had achieved cooperative goals, they were able to manage their difficulties and reassure and support each other so that they could make use of new structures.

Reducing costs is high on the agenda for many firms. Traditionally, top management has dictated cost cuts, but these often reduce the future effectiveness of the organization. Money is saved in the short term, but competitive advantage is lost in the long term. A study in a Dutch research hospital found that physicians and other members of a department who discussed conflicts cooperatively arrived at solutions that increased efficiency and reduced costs. This cooperative conflict was especially critical because the hospital's sponsoring university planned to withdraw from patient care and reduce hospital staff by twenty-five percent in three years. If the department could not decide how to make cuts, the hospital board would.

Many companies rely on performance appraisal systems to promote the development and learning of employees. Less recognized is that the utility of performance appraisal depends in large part on the effective discussion of opposing views on the employee's performance and on plans for improvement. In a study in a large telecommunications company, managers with bosses who dealt with conflicts cooperatively, rather than competitively or avoidantly, rated the quality of the feedback high, felt more motivated to work hard, were more committed to the performance appraisal, and were confident they could work well with their boss in the future.

Every organization must serve its customers. Quality service is essential for organizational effectiveness. To serve customers well, various departments and groups must coordinate and manage their conflicts. Successful sales representatives develop a network of people within their organizations and deal openly and cooperatively with their conflicts. Indeed, salespeople must manage conflict cooperatively with customers to earn repeat business. Effective conflict management throughout the organization and with customers builds an organization that serves.

Studying and discussing cooperative and competitive conflict together is a powerful way for people to break out of their ineffective conflicts. In the next chapter, Eric and Willem debate cooperation and competition and plan how together they can make their conflicts more cooperative and effective.

Discuss Conflict Handling with Your Antagonist

Guides for Action

- Distinguish between the conflict over the issue and the one over how conflicts are being managed.
- Recognize that characterizing the other as arrogant and closed-mined grows out of competitive conflict.
- Take the first steps toward discussing openly how conflicts are being managed.
- Check assumptions that the other is unwilling to improve conflict management.
- Deal with competitive, negative attitudes.
- Try to remain open-minded and fair.
- Focus on working together to improve conflict management.
- Discuss the costs of the destructive conflict and the mutual benefits of productive conflict.
- Signal that the conflict can be constructively resolved.
- Avoiding blaming and affronting social face.
- Demonstrate that you are trying to understand the other's perspective.
- Counter the negative perceptions your antagonist has of you by acting inconsistently with them.
- Empower your antagonist by offering options to chose.
- Know and be prepared to use alternatives to a negotiated agreement.

Pitfalls to Avoid

- Keep arguments rational and task-oriented, even when competitive and negative attitudes are getting in the way.
- Assume that discussing how the conflict is being managed is too personal and will escalate the conflict.
- Assume you alone must manage conflict.
- Assume your opponent alone must change.
- Believe that the conflict means that the other wants to be frustrating and mean.
- Convince yourself that your antagonist does not want to manage conflict based on indirect evidence.
- Wait for the other to make the first move to prove good intentions.

5

Learning Together

Where do you find common ground? At the point of challenge.
— *Jesse Ericson*

"Isn't this idea of cooperative conflict too idealistic?" Willem asked Eric. They were meeting to discuss the article and book on work relationships and conflict management they had agreed to read. "People aren't that rational in conflict. I've seen some pretty strange behavior."

"It's more realistic than the idea that somehow we should work without conflict," Eric said. "Cooperative conflict at least recognizes our differences, and I find that refreshing."

"But cooperative conflict has to be practical, something we can do. It should be a realistic ideal."

"I could see myself, even you, in some of those examples," Eric teased.

"I saw you in that example of how to manage conflict with a boss; you were in a position of power that you always covet," Willem teased back.

"This cooperative conflict is something different than the idea that we're supposed to be highly rational and unemotional. In the examples, people were showing their anger and frustration. That's realistic, too."

Willem paused. "It's challenging just to think how to be emotional as well as positive in conflict."

"I don't see how you can be a rational machine when you're in conflict."

"But you need to be reasonable, too. Understanding conflict is not easy."

"Let's brainstorm what cooperative conflict means," Eric began. "People respect and trust each other; they avoid insults and tricks."

"We're suppose to speak openly and directly about what is bothering us and what is on our minds. That's the part I like best," Willem laughed.

"The solving problems in cooperative conflict is the part I like best," Eric deadpanned.

"I didn't know that you would go in for something as dry as that," Willem teased.

Eric turned serious. "It doesn't seem like this cooperative conflict is really a specific strategy—it's more like an attitude, even a feeling."

"It's what the two people believe about each other and what they want to accomplish."

Eric read from the book, "In cooperation, people want each other to win; in competition they want to win and the other to lose."

"It's not so much the truth as what people believe to be true." Willem thought for a moment. "I may want us both to win, but you may think I want you to lose."

"I don't just think, I know," Eric said.

Willem laughed. "When the other person is convinced you're against him, then it makes conflict very dicey. Everything you say is taken the wrong way."

"It's much better when people believe they're working with each other, not against each other."

"What we need is to feel we're on the same side. But how can you persuade someone that you're on his side?" Willem asked.

"It's especially difficult in conflict. The book says somewhere that we should work on developing a cooperative relationship so that when the conflict comes, we believe we're allies."

"Like ourselves, we're better off when we think cooperatively," Willem said.

"If we in sales see you in support as against our getting our price and schedule confirmed, then we feel competitive. If we see you as trying to help us get the the best long-term price and schedule for the company, then we feel cooperative."

"That's where teamwork comes in, people working on common tasks, sharing work and rewards. Teams find it easier to believe they are on the same side and to talk directly about issues for mutual benefit."

Eric looked through the book. "It says here that learning to manage conflict is also a way to have a cooperative relationship. It made sense when I read it, but now it seems odd."

"The idea is a little different," Willem said as he paged through the book. "This chapter says that by studying and learning how to manage conflict together people show that they both want to improve how they're dealing with their differences. They're also actually cooperating by working together and helping each other."

"Aren't we doing that now?" Eric smiled. "We're doing something right."

For another fifteen minutes, Willem and Eric discussed and debated the value of a cooperative context, how it can be created, and how to discuss differences to reinforce a cooperative relationship. Finally, Willem said, "We should talk about how cooperative conflict applies to us. We want to get better at our dealing with our differences, right?"

"Of course." Eric knew this was the next step, yet he felt anxious and a part of him did not want to proceed.

Willem was not surprised by Eric's hesitancy; if anything, it made him plunge in more quickly. "I don't believe that we have a cooperative conflict when you surprise me with a demand for quick approval of a difficult case. It's like you think what we've done has little value and that we have nothing better to do than jump when you say jump. It's you, you, you, not us."

Although Eric realized that Willem's directness was useful, he felt somewhat put down, without any outlet for his feelings. He focused on rephrasing the issue to demonstrate that he was trying to understand Willem. "I can see that it's a nuisance when I come in and ask for special treatment. I don't like doing it, really. Let me assure you that I don't mean to imply in any way that your work is unimportant."

"Really? You even talk about how we're here to serve you, like we're servants and you're the masters."

"You are suppose to serve us," Eric said candidly.

"But it is a two-way street; we help you do your job and you help us do our job. We have to get this straight."

Eric felt tied up. He couldn't help thinking that Willem had the upper hand and was attacking him. But he wanted to avoid lashing out. He tried to listen.

"And another thing we have to get straight," Willem continued. "I remember when you came over to talk to me about how we needed to manage conflict. The idea was a good one, of course, but you came over unannounced and sprang the idea on me. Then you cracked jokes. How do you expect me to respond to that? You're not acting like you want to help me, but to surprise and distract me."

"That's going too far." Eric couldn't keep all his frustration inside.

"No, it isn't. I'm telling you something about how you deal with me that gets in the way of managing our conflicts. I thought that's what we're doing."

"Okay, okay." Eric was beginning to appreciate—even envy—Willem's style.

"When you want to talk to me about an important issue, you should call me and make an appointment. It's only reasonable."

"I just thought dropping by would be more personal and informal."

"Let me get this straight. For unimportant issues you make an appointment, and for important ones you don't."

"Putting it that way does make it sound strange. You have so many rules."

"Yes, I do have rules," Willem responded.

"But there's something to be said for being able to get together on the spur of the moment."

"Sure. But I don't like to be surprised and asked to deal with important issues on a crisis basis. I'm not being unreasonable."

"I agree it's a reasonable request," Eric said.

"And your humor?"

"I understand that you don't like me to crack jokes."

"No, that's not it. I don't like to joke when trying to discuss a serious issue."

Eric resisted a joke and a smile. "I can try not to joke when we're dealing with a conflict."

"Good."

Though he felt battered, Eric wanted to keep going. His anxiety had subsided and they were making progress. "But why haven't we developed a stronger relationship? That would make discussing our issues much less difficult."

They discussed what led them to think competitively and cooperatively for twenty minutes. They concluded that, while there were some general cooperative goals, NorTel had given them reasons to feel competitive. Their cooperative goals included a shared vision and general sense that they worked for one company, but these ideals were not strong in the fragmented, complex organization of NorTel. Their boss's management style—giving them different and opposing objectives but no help in resolving their differences— seemed to make them more competitive than cooperative.

Eric and Willem did not want to lay all the blame on the boss and the company. They were not pawns and could together strengthen their cooperation. They could redefine their groups' missions as committed to assisting each other as equals. They could help each other become more competent at managing conflict and leadership more generally. They could speak well of each other to enhance their reputations. They could meet regularly to hammer out issues for mutual benefit.

"Sometimes managing conflict and working cooperatively seem so hard, but right now they seem straightforward," Eric said. "We can do it."

"Not just the two of us, though," Willem cautioned. "We need to bring our groups along as well."

"Right. Also we should figure out a way of filling in the boss so that it makes sense to him."

"So he won't feel threatened, you mean."

"Yes." Eric paused. "We can't jump to conclusions, though. It may be that he's wanted us to solve our problems all along."

"But he didn't know how to teach us to manage our conflicts? That's possible."

"We have challenges ahead."

"Good progress, very interesting, if a little exhausting." Eric told Anthony about his discussions with Willem as they met at the gym.

"Way to go! I'm not surprised. Two reasonable people can make progress if they sit down and talk about things."

"The book and article were useful, too, because they helped us clarify our thinking and get into the issue deeper."

Seeing Eric's hesitation, Anthony asked, "Some things didn't go so well?"

"Willem is so direct."

"What did he say?"

"He was telling me not to joke when we discuss our conflicts."

"He's right, you do that. I'm so used to it that it doesn't bother me. I don't even notice anymore."

"I guess it's a bad habit." Eric was trying to accept this feedback, but he also wanted assurance.

"I'd put it this way: It doesn't work with Willem, but it works with me. But most people are not like me and haven't known you for years."

"Hmm . . . . He also said I needed to make appointments and be more formal. I suppose that's a good idea, but he was kind of rough."

"You've always been sensitive to criticism," Anthony said almost casually. "You wear your distress so we can see it."

"Does anyone else want to take a potshot at me?" Eric wanted a lighter mood.

"Hey, it's just Anthony, your old friend. Maybe you should talk about your sensitivity to criticism with Willem sometime."

"He might not even know that I'm sensitive."

"He probably does, but it might be good to get it on the table, especially because in NorTel, you manager types are all supposed to be superhuman, unemotional, and always competent and in charge. Not very realistic."

"This learning to manage conflict can be hard work."

"Never ending and never a dull moment."

Humor in Conflict

Humor and conflict go together. From Shakespeare to Norman Lear, much of our humor is based at laughing at our own and others' conflicts. We laugh at our predicaments and make jokes at the expense of other groups. We deal with low energy by teasing our colleagues to get their attention and raise the tension. Sometimes our teasing is too much and results in angry coworkers. Laughing is a way of dealing with conflicts. Some people joke and laugh as a way to avoid discussing conflicts directly. They want the issue to slip away. Sarcasm can be an attempt to overpower others and suppress conflict. But people also laugh when they want to communicate that they are enjoying the excitement of the conflict and appreciate getting involved. Laughter can be a way of saying that the conflict is not so awful and that it can be resolved effectively.

In addition to being potentially very useful for relationships and managing conflict, laughter is physically good for people. Laughter is a series of involuntary spasms of the diaphragm, which forces the breathing muscles to contract and relax quickly. The chest cavity increases, allowing the lungs to take in more oxygen and expel more carbon dioxide. Laughter exercises the lungs, increases circulation and metabolism, and gives the cardiovascular system a work out. Laughter also exercises chest, face, and abdomen muscles; these relaxing muscles lower the pulse rate and blood pressure. A hearty laugh may give up to forty-five minutes of relaxation and reduced anxiety. Laughter also releases the body's natural painkiller, endorphins.

But as Eric was finding out, laughter is doubled edged. His humor fostered mistrust and irritation when he joked while trying to discuss a serious conflict with Willem. Later, he and Willem enjoyed teasing each other as they discussed their conflicts.

Humor is best when it is intended and considered as a contribution to the relationship and, in particular, to cooperative conflict. Humor is then a sign that people are involved and committed to each other and that they are able to deal with their tensions and conflicts in a mutually beneficial way. Their relationship is so strong that even in a conflict they enjoy each other. ("We can laugh about our problems and conflicts.")

Such people use humor constructively. They do not let it interfere with open, direct discussions about serious conflict. However, they may tease and laugh competitively on small issues. ("I haven't seen checked ties and striped shirts together in some time." "It's my 1960s Minnesota look—our ex-hippie customers appreciate it much more than expensive, matched outfits.") Or they may use humor to avoid small conflicts and give way to a friend or colleague. ("Never know, I may even like baseball after the fifth game you've taken me to. Stranger things have happened.")

Relationships for Learning

Eric and Willem were learning the value of relationships for helping them become more effective at managing conflict. Together, they dug into the ideas of cooperative conflict, identified what leads to cooperative and competitive goals, and examined the behaviors that reinforce a cooperative context. Then they applied these ideas to their own conflicts. Eric also turned to Anthony for assistance. People working together as a team have important advantages in learning and applying conflict knowledge.

Cooperative Learning

David Johnson, a social psychologist, and his brother Roger Johnson, an educator, both from the University of Minnesota, have conducted and summarized research documenting the value of co-operative goals and interaction for learning. In a statistical review of over five-hundred studies, cooperative learning was found to promote higher achievement, more complex reasoning, higher levels of self-esteem, and greater feelings of social support than when people studied competitively or independently. These findings apply to adults as well as children.

Cooperative goals facilitate interaction—including open discussion of opposing views—that helps people understand such abstract, powerful ideas as cooperative conflict. People can discuss and debate issues to clarify confusions; they can critique, challenge, and probe ideas; they can connect present with past learning. In cooperative learning, people have been found to ask more questions, debate different positions, elaborate their views, and engage in problem solving, all of which help them understand and evaluate the strengths and limitations of ideas. People learn by having ideas explained and by explaining ideas. When people learn together, there is a richness to the exchange when people learn together that is not possible when they learn competitively or by themselves.

Personal Learning

Learning together is especially useful for the personal and emotional demands of understanding conflict. Cooperative conflict has important implications for our thinking and actions. It challenges our habits, asks us to think about our relationships and ourselves in new ways, and opens up possibilities of more effective behavior. Cooperative learning encourages the support, feedback, and problem solving needed for personal change.

As Eric was rediscovering, learning about the affect one has on others can be hard emotional work. Willem and Anthony gave him direct feedback on his actions and how they saw and reacted to his behavior. But this feedback was not simple to understand and use. Part of Eric wanted to deny and downplay the feedback, which seemed to suggest that he appeared ineffective. To an achievement-oriented person like Eric, this suggestion implied that he was rejected and found wanting as a person. In the short term, he would have found it easier to shrug off the idea as something said in the heat of a conflict and to seek reassurance.

Willem and Anthony persisted and offered help and support so that Eric could see the feedback as well intentioned and useful. They communicated acceptance of him even though they saw weaknesses in his conflict style. Eric gradually overcame his fears that he was generally seen as incompetent and unacceptable by his peers and friends.

Personal change also requires applying ideas and feedback. Friends, colleagues, and family members can provide the emotional and problem-solving support needed to translate the theory of cooperative conflict and insights about one's behavior into personal change. Willem and Eric together identified concrete new ways they could discuss their differences and improve their conflict skills. These solutions needed to be specific to them. If Willem were a different person, joking and formal meetings might not have been important issues.

Studying and thinking individually would have been much less productive for developing solutions. Eric and Willem would have felt powerless for neither could decide or impose solutions on the other. People in conflict are often pessimistic about whether they can persuade their conflict partners to adopt a new approach. But by working together they can strengthen each individual's abilities and improve their joint conflict management.

Learning Together

Guides for Action

- Commit to learning to manage conflict and to developing other cooperative skills.
- Discuss cooperative conflict with conflict partners.
- Exchange ideas and opinions freely as you learn basic conflict management ideas.
- Use managing conflict skills to learn about conflict.
- Debate the uses and limits of cooperative conflict.
- Use cooperative conflict to analyze your present and past conflicts.
- Give descriptive, useful feedback on how you and your conflict partners manage conflict cooperatively.
- Provide the acceptance and emotional support needed to use feedback.
- Brainstorm how you could make your conflicts more cooperative and effective.
- Implement and assess the success of your plans.
- Use humor to strengthen cooperative relationships.

Pitfalls to Avoid

- Assume you know the theory of cooperative conflict because you read about it.
- Equate using new terms with understanding ideas.
- Believe that reading and talking about cooperative conflict will make it happen.
- Badger people into accepting cooperative conflict as their guide.
- Tell people to change.
- Give feedback and then run away.
- Make fun of people's weaknesses.
- Use sarcasm to maintain power and control.

6

Broadening the Learning Network

*We cannot live only for ourselves. A thousand fibers connect us with
our fellow-men; and along those fibers, as sympathetic threads our actions run as causes, and they come back to us as effects.*
—Herman Melville

"I like being direct," Eric said. He had just entered Willem's office.

"It's Mr. Conflict at work defending the innocent and protecting
the helpless, I presume," Willem teased.

"Yes, people like me and people like you." Eric and Willem enjoyed laughing together and knowing that, rather than burdens,
their differences and tensions made their interactions livelier and
more fun.

Eric described how he had summarized their progress to Wendy
Chow, the human resources manager who had suggested the book
and article they had used to study cooperative conflict together. "I
told her that we saw great potential in this idea of cooperative conflict for ourselves, our groups, and the whole company and that we
wanted her assistance."

"The more you and I have talked, the more clear it is that NorTel
needs cooperative conflict. Think of the wasted energy and emotion
because of how the different business units fight each other. We're
too busy fighting each other to worry about the competition, much
less the customer."

Eric liked to see Willem so focused and he added, "Those crazy
things that come from the executive committee. They move groups

and people on the organization chart like pawns, but they give them no help in actually working together better. Everyone feels besieged."

"Then they think if they get us all together and shout that we believe in quality and customers, great things will happen."

"Its frustrates us and hurts the bottom line. Frankly, it doesn't make me feel very optimistic about my or anyone's future here at NorTel."

"Wendy must have been delighted that you wanted to do something," Willem said.

"Not really. She told me about the programs they've already set for this year. She went on and on about how they've assessed the company's training needs and have made their one-year, two-year and five-year plans."

"She doesn't get it; she doesn't see the value of cooperative conflict. That's the same old line about how professional they are and how they plan for the future and we don't," Willem said.

"Exactly. Before I would have just thought to myself, 'Let her dig her own grave,' but after talking about conflict management and seeing your direct style in action, I just said, 'Listen, there's a big gulf between your department and the line managers. Here's a chance to become a real part of the company. Don't blow it.'"

"That's direct."

"She was startled, but to her credit, she hung in there and heard me out."

"Did she admit there's a problem with her department's place in the company?"

"Not in so many words, but she did say they want to be seen as more helpful, as a department that takes care of its customers. At the end, she said we could count on her, but we should remember that her department has other plans and restraints."

"Good result. She'll come in handy, especially if we need to hire outside trainers. If she got excited, she could help bring cooperative conflict corporate-wide."

"Talking with her got me all pumped up again about managing conflict. It would be great to have fewer stupid decisions and inflexible policies and to get people together to improve our products and services. It can really give this company a spirit, an excitement that we don't have. We get paid well enough, our jobs are secure, at least for now, and the company makes some money. But we need more than that."

"The company does have sort of a fairyland quality about it," Willem said. "But this, too, will pass, once the regulators let others into our markets. Life will be different at NorTel in five years, though I'm not sure exactly how."

"You know it, I know it—but do other people know it?"

"They do, but no one knows quite what to do."

"That's why I'm so excited about cooperative conflict. It can help us now and also help us prepare for the unpredictable future. It can give us the spirit that we 're getting better, we're learning. It's good if the two of us manage our conflicts, but think of the power if all of us are learning to deal with conflicts. We'd all be more productive."

"You're preaching to the converted. But NorTel's not prepared for it. People have swept problems under the rug for so long that you're asking them to do nearly a 180-degree turnaround by dealing with all those problems they have tried to ignore."

"That's what's so exciting."

Willem and Eric, though they agreed that cooperative conflict would be very useful, debated whether other managers and employees would welcome a program to learn to manage their conflicts.

"Okay, let's say you're right that cooperative conflict is a very big leap for NorTel," Eric said. "Let's start small with our groups and division."

"Makes sense. Our success would be evidence that may even convince skeptics. We should do it. You take the lead and I'll back you up. You're much more convincing that NorTel can really change its ways."

"We have an immediate stumbling block—our boss. He'll look over his glasses and ask skeptical questions. I guess there's no way to avoid him." Eric was suddenly pessimistic.

"You expected that getting people to learn to manage conflict would be without conflict?" Willem teased. "We can't expect our people to get involved if the boss might hold it against them."

"I'm not sure how you see it, but I think Hugh is one of those good-hearted people who have been sweeping problems under the rug."

"What's more, he thinks he's good at dealing with people. I'll let you break the news. You like being direct."

"But you have much more experience," Eric teased back.

They discussed how Eric could approach their boss, Hugh Thompson, directly yet cautiously to brief him on their progress and ask for his encouragement. They decided that Eric needed to give the boss a concise overview of cooperative conflict backed up with concrete steps.

"Interesting topic, Eric, this conflict idea," Hugh began. "I just glanced through that article you gave me, and there's certainly lots of conflict in the world. On the other hand, we need to be balanced here and keep on our business target."

Eric thought to himself, "The polite brushoff, a skill he's been mastering for twenty years at NorTel." Eric was prepared and replied without irritation, "Agreed, and keeping on target is going to be more and more difficult." Typically, Eric would have launched into a spirited defense of his idea, and Hugh would have raised objections and found holes in his logic. This time, Eric went more slowly.

Hugh paused, expecting Eric to continue. Eric, he thought, was always able to talk. His role was to harness Eric's energy and enthusiasm. "We can't get sidetracked. This is not a high-tech, high-flying company; it's a solid company with solid technology."

"Good people, too," Eric said without sarcasm.

"We have to be careful about how we spend our money and time."

"Agreed. But think of the time and money wasted when we don't handle conflicts well and make bad decisions, spend our time brooding and working against each other. Think of all the time wasted because of poorly managed conflict. Time is money. Learning to manage conflict is an investment that continues to pay off."

"Interesting. But what I'm getting at is that I don't want us to get distracted with new slogans."

"I don't either. We need lots of focus. To get that focus we need the drive, the spirit, to work on something important but immediate and practical enough to get our hands on. We'd all benefit from learning to manage our conflict and getting the company prepared for the uncertain future."

"I suppose, but we can't have people screaming and arguing all day."

"We want people debating when's it's time for discussion and agreeing and getting on with it when a decision has been made. Wouldn't life be better around here without second-guessing?" Second-guessing was one of Hugh's pet peeves.

"It's awful. It's like all the debate happens after the decision."

Eric felt he was on a roll. "And wouldn't we be better off if people discussed their differences rather than gossiping and complaining about each other behind their backs?" Gossiping was another pet peeve.

"People should be more responsible and not gossip."

"But telling them they should be responsible doesn't stop hallway backstabbing."

"Yes, I know. So you think if we manage our conflict all these problems would disappear?"

"The problems and conflicts wouldn't disappear, but we could be much more direct and open about our differences and not push them into the corridors. Then we could get some resolutions, some progress."

Hugh did not want to disappoint Eric; he would prefer to dissuade or deflect him. But he could feel the cold, disbelieving eyes of his boss and peers when they heard what Eric was doing and put him on the spot by asking him to explain Eric's idea. Those engineers didn't have a clue about conflict management—even the idea of teamwork seemed strange to them. Hugh was looking for a graceful way out of this situation. "Give me some examples of what you'd do."

Eric explained that he wanted his people to study cooperative conflict and together plan how they could use it for the department.

"Sounds vague," Hugh said. "There must be something concrete."

"There's a procedure called advocacy teams to make decisions. One group takes the pro side and another group the con side; each side develops their arguments and collects facts and ideas that support their positions. Then they come together and debate the issue fully."

"A little odd, but perhaps not worse than the way we make decisions now. What do you do when everyone remains divided?"

"That's what happens now. Decisions are made, then people complain about them. It would be better to have them divided before a decision so that they can put together their ideas and become united behind our decision." Eric outlined additional plans.

Doubting that Eric could be talked out of this idea and not feeling that he could defend a no, Hugh began to console himself that this was not as impractical as some of Eric's schemes. "The CEO keeps talking about empowering people. Perhaps this managing conflict is part of that. Could you write me a one-page memo defining what you're doing for my records? Go ahead and try your idea for a while and see how it goes."

"Sounds reasonable. After we've tried using conflict to make a decision, can I come back and let you know the results? Experience can help us get a better understanding of cooperative conflict."

"Good. Keep me informed. I'll try to read that article."

"You may even beat me tonight," Eric laughed as he and Anthony were warming up for their evening run.

"I guess this rescuing a company is tiring business," Anthony said with warm sarcasm. Eric had recapped his discussions with Willem and Hugh.

"Just trying to pump up the organization a bit. Seriously, a steady, more or less guaranteed profit sounds awfully good—and its better than a guaranteed loss—but it has made us sleepy. When you get down to it, money is not enough."

"Spoken like a man with a steady income. But I believe you anyway."

"Your mention of rescuing made me think that perhaps I'm on too big an ego trip, trying to get my picture on the front of one of those business magazines. This is suppose to be *cooperative* conflict. The book said something about the best way to manage conflict is together and the best way to learn to manage conflict is together."

"Cut yourself a break, Eric. Are you working just for your own benefit? No. Are you trying to show up people? No. You just told me about how you've been talking and involving Hugh and Willem. It certainly doesn't sound like they think you're just doing your thing. It seems to me you're providing leadership."

"Just checking. I'm glad you see it that way. Now, on to victory."

Involving Others

Eric and Willem sensed the potential for innovation, customer service, and human development if the people at NorTel would manage their conflicts together. They were enthusiastic about their experience and wanted to share it with others. They were convinced that learning to manage conflict is much more effective when done together.

Eric and Willem realized that, in addition to promoting the company, they personally would be more effective if others at NorTel were also learning to manage conflict cooperatively. Eric and Willem would be able to work together more effectively to the extent that employees in their own departments used cooperative conflict. If other managers also took an open, cooperative approach to their conflicts, Eric and Willem would be more successful and less frustrated. They sought their boss's support because they wanted their work on cooperative conflict to be seen as contributing to their potential as future executives, not to be held against them. They wanted their boss and other executives to realize that they were working for the good of the company.

Eric and Willem appreciated that everyone could find learning to manage conflict rewarding and fulfilling for their work and life outside of work. The more people at NorTel committed to managing their conflicts, the more empowering and successful the program would be. People would be confident that their conflict partners were also trying to deal with conflicts openly and honestly and encouraging each other to develop these abilities. The more you give conflict management away, the more you get back.

Improving conflict management could be an important aspect of NorTel's shared vision. It had immediate payoff, but it also realistically prepared the company for the future. Cooperative conflict could become a common framework that NorTel managers and employees used to guide their joint efforts. Cooperative conflict could help them analyze their present ways of collaborating and decide how to strengthen them. It is ironic that learning to manage conflict unites an organization.

Eric and Willem were trying to make a difference, but Eric was concerned about his own motivation. Too often he had seen bosses restructure the division just to be seen as doing something important and leaving their mark. Top executives had taken their companies to bankruptcy in ego-driven acquisitions. But Anthony helped him allay these concerns. Eric was working to leave his mark, but he was doing that with other people. These people would not be forced, but through discussion and debate would be asked to consider how learning to manage conflict would promote their own and the company's interests. Productive leadership occurs within a context of collaborative effort and cooperative conflict.

Conflict to Form a Network

Building a coalition of people committed to learning to manage conflict, like other important tasks, requires conflict management. Although some people may immediately see the rationale, many others will have doubts, misgivings, and objections. These conflicts are not problems in themselves. Indeed, they gave Eric and Willem a chance to practice and demonstrate their conflict skills.

To develop a plan, Willem and Eric discussed their opposing views about how ready NorTel was for learning conflict management. They would begin with themselves and their own department. In that way, they could demonstrate their conviction and develop their knowledge, understanding, and skills in cooperative conflict. Their successful experiences could demonstrate the value of cooperative conflict and ways to implement it. Their failures could highlight barriers and pitfalls to avoid.

Their discussions also made it clear that they should try to involve Hugh and Wendy as partners. Eric and Willem told them directly of their plans and intentions, asked for their assistance, and promised to keep them informed about their experiences. In this way, Hugh and Wendy would be on the inside of their experiment to understand cooperative conflict better and would see how concretely it can be implemented and used effectively. If Eric and Willem had acted alone, Hugh and Wendy might have felt suspicious that perhaps Eric and Willem were trying to show them up. Hugh and Wendy might have become enemies, not partners in learning to manage conflict.

Eric used cooperative conflict in discussions with both Wendy and Hugh. He discussed the learning conflict program directly and showed that he wanted to develop a program that would serve their interests as well as his own. However, the particular approach and strategies he employed were quite different. With Wendy, he was blunt and confrontational. With Hugh, he was diffident and cautious.

Cooperative conflict suggests how managers can be both credible and flexible. Successful managers have long recognized that they must use strategies appropriate to the situation. Eric was credible in using a cooperative conflict approach, but he adjusted it to fit the personalities of his conflict partners and their relationship with him.

Cooperative conflict is an elegant, powerful way to analyze organizations and act in them, but it is also abstract. People have to understand cooperative conflict well enough to adapt it to the personalities and the relationships of people as well as to the restraints and demands of the situation. No simple formulas are universally effective. People must create specific strategies and make wise choices. In the next section, we see how people use conflict knowledge to make effective choices and create new ways to handle their diverse conflicts.

Building a Learning Network

Guides for Action

- Give conflict management away so you get more back.
- Use conflict cooperatively to unite your company.
- Involve others so that they become partners in enhancing the organization's conflict management.
- Manage the conflict needed to build a network for learning.
- Use dissenting opinions to create more effective plans to enhance conflict skills.

Pitfalls to Avoid

- Seek to learn conflict management as a competitive edge over the people you must work with.
- Assume that your personal learning is enough.
- Imply that you are superior because you are learning to manage conflict.
- Force people to learn to manage conflict.
- Assume objections are mean-spirited barriers.
- Try to change the whole organization overnight.
- Give up changing anything.

PART THREE

Extending Conflict Competence

When men think and believe in one set of symbols and act in ways which are contrary to their professed and conscious ideas, confusion and insincerity are bound to result.

—John Dewey

Conflict is a rich, complex experience that stimulates our thinking, involves our interests and goals, and generates strong emotions. Learning to manage challenges us to elaborate our ideas as we understand others', to assert our goals as we respond to the aspirations of others, and to express our feelings to help others express theirs. Through such efforts we learn more about the obstacles and opportunities before our colleagues, friends, and ourselves.

Chapter 7 shows how opposing positions can be debated to dig into issues and understand problems, create and examine alternatives, and make high-quality decisions. Chapter 8 reviews how a manager can mediate to help employees confront their differences and negotiate a settlement. Anger is the most difficult to manage feeling in conflict, but, as shown in chapter 9, well-managed anger contributes to meaningful cooperative conflict.

7

Making Decisions to Solve Problems

It's a serious mistake for any leader to be surrounded by sycophants. . . .
The stronger and more self-assured a leader is the more likely he or she
is to seek diversity of advice. If you are insecure or don't have confi-
dence in yourself, then you're apt to listen to a narrow range of advice.
I deliberately chose advisers with disparate points of view.

—Jimmy Carter

"We could do it together," Eric said to Willem. They had been complaining about the latest memo from the executive committee. In its
work to revise NorTel's price policy, the committee had asked Eric
to detail the sales group's position and Willem the marketing support's position.

"Wouldn't it be easier just to change the introductions of the
memos we sent six months ago?" Willem asked.

"Even though we're close to the customer and the marketplace,
they still don't seem to take our suggestions too seriously. Then we
don't take their requests too seriously."

"There's a balance," Willem sighed. "I have an idea. Perhaps we
could use this problem to get our groups thinking in terms of cooperative conflict." They had each introduced the value of managing
conflict to their groups and had made readings available. But they
were unsure how they could get their groups to manage conflict cooperatively.

"Hugh suggested I begin with a structured way to use conflict to
make a decision."

"Do you mean advocacy teams?" Willem asked. "That's where

we assign groups to take opposite sides, give them time to get prepared, and then have them argue their opposing positions, right?"

"Yes. Your group could take the maintain prices position and my group the lower our prices one. That would be logical."

"Sounds like the sparks would fly. But we should mix up our people. Let them get to know each other and defend the other side. That'll be good for them."

"But will they do it?"

Eric and Willem discussed how they might introduce and structure the advocacy team approach of cooperative conflict to solve problems and make decisions. They were excited about the prospects and glad they could rely on each other's help and enthusiasm.

Eric and Willem reminded the people in their groups that an effective price structure was vital for NorTel's adaptation to the changing marketplace. They had an opportunity to influence pricing policy by making a cogent, persuasive, and useful recommendation to the executive committee.

"Willem and I believe that the way to take advantage of this opportunity is for us to use cooperative controversy to dig into the issues and create a solution that can really help the executive committee get a handle on what to do. The committee should be grateful because it's trying to grapple with new strategies for NorTel in a new marketplace."

"Our plan is to divide into two groups and assign one the position that we should maintain our prices and the other the position that we should lower them." Willem outlined the basic steps of advocacy teams.

Advocacy Team Guides

Phase 1: Select a problem that warrants a comprehensive evaluation. Identify the major alternative positions.

Phase 2: Assign opposing positions to teams. Provide resources teams can use to gather arguments and information for their position.

Phase 3: Each team presents its arguments. Listen open-mindedly and challenge constructively.

Phase 4: Teams rephrase the opposing arguments. Put into their own words the ideas, logic, and facts given by the other side.

Phase 5: The team as a whole strives to create an integrated solution. Examine all the evidence and arguments to reach a consensus decision based on current knowledge. Be prepared to recycle through advocacy teams to develop and refine the decision.

Phase 6: The team implements the decision. Persist and follow through with the agreement.

Phase 7: The team reflects and learns from its experience. Discuss strengths and areas to improve.

Eric could sense misgivings among some people. He did not know quite how to respond, but he saw in Willem's face that they should press forward. "We have listed who belongs to which group," Eric said as he handed out lists. "The timetable is that you have one week to get prepared and the debate will occur here next week, same time and same place. Any questions?"

After they gave the groups time to get organized and find a time for their first meeting, Eric and Willem discussed what they had to do next. They were concerned because there was not more overt enthusiasm about the advocacy teams nor more than a couple questions of clarification. Perhaps people were just getting used to the new procedure.

Two days later, Nick met with Eric to talk about his group's position. "We've met and done some preliminary work, but we're a little confused," he began. "Some of us don't really agree with the position that prices should be maintained. But somehow you want us not to believe what we do believe."

"No, we're not asking you to believe something you don't. But we want you to argue the other position. You can use your ideas about why prices should be lower to develop arguments for why prices should be maintained."

"So it's not a mistake that I'm in this group. We were also wondering whether we all debate our position or assign a spokesperson."

"I assume that one person will present the opening position and then others will enter into the open debate part of the discussion. Certainly we want everyone involved." Eric hoped that the advocacy teams were working. "Are you enjoying this way of discussing?"

"Sure. Nothing like a little change to stir things up. We were just a little confused about some of the details."

"No problem. Glad you stopped in."

On the scheduled day of the debate, both groups seemed eager to begin. There was good-natured teasing.

Eva laughed, "We hope you have some fancy overheads to mask the lack of hard facts to support your position."

Albert countered, "We'll leave boring facts to you. We have truth on our side."

"We are—we think—glad you're in a fighting mood," Willem said. "But, of course, this discussion is not a test of manhood, but a way to get at the best recommendations and decisions."

"Don't take all the fun out of it," Nick shouted out. "We're here for victory!"

Both groups had selected outspoken people to present their opening positions. Nick outlined the defense of maintaining prices with fanfare and humor. He first argued why the market would respond well to the present prices and then how these prices were needed internally to support investment in new products vital for long-term success. Elizabeth, from marketing support, used slides to dramatize the invasion of NorTel's markets by new rivals. These new firms were hungry, lean, and flexible, but they had one weakness that NorTel could exploit: They were undercapitalized and could not endure a long price war.

The open debate began hesitantly, but quickly grew in intensity and volume. Eric was relieved that people were getting highly involved in the discussion. Surely, they were grappling with this complex issue and something good would come out of it. Willem was laughing and enjoying the drama and humor.

After thirty minutes of open debate, Eric asked the groups to drop their assigned position and try to integrate the ideas and information into a common recommendation. Here, too, the discussion began haltingly with a few jokes. Albert said, "Only a coward would change his mind now." Leslie teased, "I can see where you men would have difficulty changing your mind—you did say '*his* mind,' didn't you?"

The joking seemed to reflect a reluctance to discard their assigned position. Once they had defended one view, it was not easy for them to agree publicly to opposing arguments. As Nick said, "Before I believed in lowering prices, now I want to argue that we must maintain them."

But as people rephrased and pointed out the value of arguments by the other group, the discussion turned to how to integrate the arguments to form a common recommendation.

There were compelling arguments on both sides and no obvious resolution. Elizabeth said, "Now I can appreciate why the executive committee appears so indecisive. It's a tough problem. It only seems easy if you don't think too much about it."

"It's a problem that involves everything," Rudy said. "We can't consider prices apart from our more general plans. We in marketing may know what is happening with customers, but pricing has to be considered in light of R&D, long-term capital spending plans, and so on."

"Right. If we promise our customers long-term relationships and commit ourselves to developing products that will serve their future needs as well, then we can charge higher prices," Albert said.

"We also have to decide how we're going to relate to our competitors. Are we going to take advantage of their undercapitalization to wage war on them, as I said earlier, or are we going to be good citizens and try to let us all live?" asked Elizabeth.

"So we won't be able to say much to the executive committee?" Eric wondered aloud.

"We have things to say," Eva interjected. "I think we could write a few interesting pages that may not be decisive, but will show that we have thought about the issues and give the executive committee food for thought."

"We should say we need a forum where we can debate this issue with other areas at NorTel," Nick added. "We could hash out ideas with the R&D and field people. We need everyone's input and need to get everyone on the same wavelength."

"Why not advocacy teams for the whole company?" Elizabeth suggested.

"So you found the advocacy team method useful, even though we have not made a final decision." Eric was happy and relieved that the experiment was an apparent success.

"I feel I have a less simplistic understanding of the issue, and that's good," Nick said.

"And we have a better view of how we can work toward a resolution," Albert said.

"Where should we go from here?" Eric asked Willem.

"Perhaps Nick and Eva can summarize our findings by drafting a memo to the executive committee," Willem responded.

Nick and Eva nodded in agreement. Eva said, "We'll send around a draft for comments and, unless there's some basic disagreement, we'll incorporate the comments into a final version. How's that?"

"Good. Eric and I want to get some feedback about the advocacy team method and how we structured it," Willem said.

There was again hesitation and silence. Then Albert said, "You guys are full of surprises."

"Do you like being surprised?" Eric asked.

"It's fun to try something different and, as you've seen, I like to mix things up," Nick said.

"I was confused at first about the procedures," Albert said. "I suppose it happens when trying something new."

"Perhaps we could have had more discussion when you introduced it," Elizabeth said. "We were hit with the idea and before we had a chance to react or ask questions about it, the meeting ended."

"Our group sort of groped along trying to figure what we were doing," Rudy said.

"We asked for questions," Willem said directly.

"But we didn't know enough to ask an intelligent question," Rudy said.

"Who wants to sound dumb by asking a dumb question like, 'What do you mean?'" Elizabeth said, to laughter. "It was as if you were highly committed to using the procedure and didn't really want to talk about it."

"We were committed," Willem said. "We wanted to expose you to each other and to managing conflict. We didn't want a vote on whether we should or not."

"Fair enough," Eva said. "But we just wanted to make sure that we understood your plan."

"We had difficulty getting productive fast because we had to get to know people from the other group," Rudy said. "But after we got started, it was fun having new people to work with."

People made additional suggestions. Perhaps instead of having one side debate the other, one person from each side could pair to debate the issue. That method would make sure everyone was involved. They wanted to get better at listening to the other side's position and showing the other side that they were listening. Writing down the other group's arguments on an overhead could give them a disciplined way to listen.

The next day, Eric sought Willem out to discuss their experiment with advocacy teams. "Not bad, quite good," Willem said.

"I really enjoyed watching them mix it up," Eric said.

"We have to figure out some way that we can get in there too. Why should they have all the fun?"

"I like their comments about writing down the other arguments and getting more involvement."

"I can see how we can adjust and fine tune our procedures."

Eric turned more serious. "We should have gotten more discussion, more conflict, when we first proposed the idea of advocacy teams."

"I guess they would have been less confused."

"It's like we want them to disagree with each other, but not with us."

"I can see where we could have done things better. But I don't take it too hard. We didn't promise them perfection."

"Live and learn," Eric commented. "There's always something to learn about leading a team and managing conflict."

"Always."

"One thing I learned is that we can be both directive and participative."

"How's that?"

"We can be directive by saying we want them to use conflict and advocacy teams to make a recommendation on prices, but we can be participative by asking for their ideas and suggestions about how we should actually do it."

Willem added, "We can be participative by having them discuss our recommendation on prices, but we can be directive in challenging their conclusions."

"What's consistent is that we're managing our conflicts cooperatively. That's what gives us credibility."

Experimenting with Advocacy Teams

Hugh encouraged Eric and Willem to use a structured approach to introduce managing conflict. The experience of using advocacy teams could help the marketing people understand the idea of cooperative conflict and how they could use it. Rather than relying only on asking everyone to speak their minds, structuring advocacy teams and assigning them different positions is a defined, thorough way to develop constructive, conflictful discussion to analyze a problem and create and evaluate alternatives. The major phases can be separated into seven steps.

Step 1: A problem important enough to warrant the time and resources needed to explore it comprehensively is identified. Simple, unimportant problems do not deserve extensive exploration and take time and attention away from significant issues. Focusing on unimportant issues can demoralize and frustrate. Short advocacy team procedures are used to begin to explore major issues or to resolve less significant ones.

Step 2: Advocacy teams are formed, and each one is assigned a major alternative. The teams are given the time and resources to find the supporting facts, information, evidence, and reasons for their alternative. They plan how they can present their arguments so that everyone is well aware of the strengths of their position. Their goal is not to win the debate by getting their position accepted, but they still want to present their arguments forcefully and thoroughly so that their position is seriously considered.

Step 3: Both teams present their arguments and position fully and persuasively. In this free discussion, each team develops its own arguments, advocates its position, defends it against refutation, and counters opposing arguments. The team members take notes and challenge inadequate facts and reasoning.

Step 4: The teams open-mindedly listen to and then present the other's position. They rephrase the other's position and arguments to demonstrate that they have paid attention and understood.

Throughout the discussion, they remember that the purpose is for the whole group to develop as strong a position as possible.

Step 5: Teams together strive to create an integrated decision. The subgroups drop their assigned positions and use all the facts and arguments identified to reach a general agreement on the best course of action. People change their minds because of the logic and evidence, not because others are more powerful or argue more loudly. The decision reflects the best joint judgment.

Step 6: The group as a whole approaches management and others to make and implement its decision. Making a decision in an organization is more than getting the right answer. Decisions are not puzzles to be solved; they are part of the stream of working and managing. The solution must be accepted and implemented, its impact assessed, and new problems identified.

Step 7: The members of the group reflect on their use of conflict to make decisions. Though advocacy teams can be exciting, involving and worthwhile, they are not easy. It can be tempting to fall back into the typical mode of trying to dominate and "win" by getting one's position accepted. Team members can easily get caught up in believing they are in a debate to prove they are right and the other is wrong. They have to remind themselves that what counts is not who was right at first but that the team is right at the end.

The advocacy teams procedure should be used flexibly and efficiently to fit the issue and circumstances. The decision to acquire a large company may deserve extensive research and repeated discussions over weeks before people feel informed and confident about a decision. But advocacy teams can be used for twenty minutes at a meeting to get people thinking about an important issue or to solve

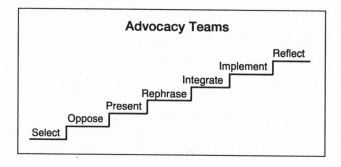

a relatively minor one. For example, rather than just asking people at the regular management meeting whether the company should follow a price reduction by a competitor, advocacy teams can be used to generate discussion and ideas and to move the group to a resolution.

Building Confidence and Competence

Eric and Willem's readings and experiences had helped them understand what cooperative conflict could do and its basic character. To introduce the idea to the people they worked with, they had talked with them about the value of managing conflict and had provided readings. Now they wanted the marketing people to experience cooperative conflict through the procedure of advocacy teams. But Eric, Willem, and the marketing people had to learn how to use advocacy teams effectively.

Eric and Willem risked looking foolish and ineffectual by using advocacy teams. Experimenting with advocacy teams was risky in a conservative company like NorTel—especially for Eric, because he was a newcomer with ambitions to move up. Fortunately, Eric could turn to Willem for ideas and support in developing and carrying out a plan of action. People in the sales and support groups also had to develop their skills to elaborate their views and listen to opposing arguments.

Advocacy teams are a tool for developing cooperative conflict, but they do not insure it. It is tempting to fall back into the typical mode of trying to dominate and win by getting one's position accepted. People easily get caught up in proving they are right and the other wrong. They have to stay focused on using conflict to pursue their common goals more effectively.

The Dynamics of Cooperative Conflict in Decision Making

State and Explain Your Position

As they begin to disagree over a problem, decision makers with cooperative goals state and explain their own positions and ideas. They identify their positions and use facts, information, and theories to validate their theses and provide a logical structure that links the facts to the conclusion. They share new information and present their ideas and rationales. As they elaborate, they can understand their own position more fully. Often people appreciate their own positions, assume that their positions are superior, and want to prove that their ideas are "right" and therefore should be accepted.

As the conflict is engaged, other people press and explain their views. Proponents may feel frustrated and argue their positions and develop their arguments more completely and forcefully. They repeat old and add new information, present more ideas, and elaborate on their positions.

Question and Understand Opposing Views

In the clash of opposing ideas and positions, people explore and refute each other's arguments. They critique and point out weaknesses and possible strengths in the arguments. They rebut counterarguments and elaborate, but they also come to doubt the wisdom and correctness of their own position. The ideas and logic of others cause people to question whether their original position is as useful and sensible as they had assumed.

People become uncertain about the validity of their original thesis. When faced with this conflict, they actively search for new information. They read more relevant material, gather new information, and ask others for information. To understand the opposing position more thoroughly, they question their opponents to clarify their positions and rephrase their arguments.

Because of their curiosity, people consider and evaluate the arguments, reasoning, and facts that support alternative positions. They can take the perspective of their opponents, anticipate how their opponents might think about future issues, and identify the kind of reasoning opponents like to employ.

Integrate and Create Options

The elaboration and exploration leave people open-minded and knowledgeable about the issue. They have approached the issue from several perspectives and are not rigidly fixed to their own. In

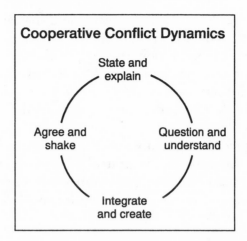

making decisions, people generally use inductive reasoning, in which they use available information to jump to a conclusion. These conclusions must be held tentatively because new information and ideas can be used to revise and improve the conclusions.

Decision makers in cooperative conflict synthesize different ideas and facts into new positions. They sense new patterns and new ways to integrate ideas. They incorporate others' information and reasoning into their own and form new attitudes and judgments. They develop positions responsive to several points of view and use more mature ways of thinking.

Agree and Shake

The dynamics of cooperative conflict result in high-quality, innovative solutions and agreements. The mix and clash of the discussion create new positions not previously considered. These positions combine the arguments and perspectives of several people in elegant ways.

Controversy encourages people to adopt more adequate ways of reasoning and to gain a deeper understanding of the problem. The increase in the number and quality of ideas and the higher levels of stimulation facilitate creativity.

Controversy is critical for successful participation in which people "own" and feel committed to decisions. People are satisfied and feel they have benefited from the discussion. They enjoy the excitement, feel aroused by the challenges of the conflict, and develop positive attitudes toward the experience. They are committed to the new agreements and positions because they understand how they are related to their own interests and positions and why the adopted position is superior to their original one.

Cooperative controversy also fosters a comraderie that reinforces commitment to the group's position. People have fully voiced their opinions, listened to each other, and enjoyed the excitement of disagreeing together. They feel better about themselves and about their team members.

The rewards of cooperative conflict in problem solving are very rich. They are much more than proving that one is right or that one's position should dominate. Constructive controversy stimulates thinking and results in effective solutions and strengthened work relationships.

Procedures for Cooperative Conflict in Decision Making

It is critical for managers and employees to aim for open discussions of opposing ideas within cooperation. In addition to advocacy teams, they can turn to other ways to develop these productive controversies.

Establish Cooperative Context

Commit to a common task. Effective decision makers want one effective decision that will promote their shared vision for the group and the company. Controversy can help them create the solution that will best promote their common interests.

Share rewards. Effective decision makers realize that they will be rewarded to the extent that the group is successful. Financial rewards, evaluations, and prestige are given for the group's success, not for independent work, appearing better than others, or proving that one is right. Rewards for success are shared; shared responsibility for failure is accepted.

Convey cooperative expectations. Effective decision makers communicate that they are committed to working for a solution that benefits all. Efforts to pursue individual objectives at others' expense should be discouraged.

Show personal regard. Effective decision makers believe they are accepted and valued as persons even though others criticize their ideas. They should listen to everyone's ideas respectfully and criticize these ideas rather than attack an individual's motivation and personality. Insults or implications that challenge another's integrity, intelligence, and motives should be avoided. Disagreement with another's current position should be accompanied by communication of interest and acceptance.

State and Explain Your Position

Develop an atmosphere of openness. Everyone should be encouraged to express opinions, doubts, uncertainties, and hunches. Ideas should not be dismissed because they first appear too unusual, impractical, or undeveloped. Affirmation of the right to dissent and of free speech reduces fears of retribution for speaking out.

Structure conflict. In addition to advocacy teams, one person can be assigned the role of a devil's advocate who makes critical evaluations of what appears to be the group's solution. Managers can actively encourage various viewpoints and assure others that they are not rigidly fixed to their present position. Requiring consensus decision making encourages full participation and allows people with doubts to speak out. Majority vote can degenerate into attempts to get a majority and force that decision on others.

Include heterogeneous members. People who differ in background, expertise, opinions, outlook, and organizational position are likely to disagree. Independent thinkers and people outside the department and organization make controversy more likely. For example, Pacific Gas & Electric decided that although environmentalists blocked some of their projects in the 1970s, the company had learned from them. Now it seeks dialogue with environmentalists inside and outside the company.

Question and Understand Opposing View

Ask questions. In cooperative conflict, people want to hear each other's arguments and reasoning directly. They explore opposing positions and try to understand the logic and facts that support them. They avoid pretending to understanding.

Conduct research. Decision makers should read the articles and materials that the opposing side is using to defend its positions.

They should visit sites and interview people who believe in and are using opposing ideas.

Influence and be open to influence. Decision makers should try to influence each other, but avoid dominating. Controversy requires people to persuade, inform, and convince to make the discussion stimulating and involving. People should have the conviction and willingness to argue their positions forcefully and to persuade, but they should avoid dominating and coercion. They should say, "I want you to consider this seriously" and "You'll probably find this convincing," not "You must accept this point" and "You have no choice but to agree." There should be give and take, not dominance or passivity.

Demonstrate understanding. Decision makers continually should put themselves in each other's shoes to understand the opposing arguments. They can show their understanding by accurately paraphrasing opposing ideas and thereby conveying acceptance and interest in another as a person while disagreeing.

Integrate and Create Options

Strive for win–win, cooperative solutions. Decision makers should say "We're all in this together" and "Let's see a solution that's good for everyone," not "I'm right, and you're wrong." Decision makers should avoid looking for winners and losers and instead focus on a productive solution to the common problem.

Combine ideas. Rather than assuming that there are only two mutually incompatible solutions, people in cooperative conflict try to integrate parts of the positions, ideas, and facts of all sides to invent an array of possible decisions.

Use rational arguments. People reason logically, listen open-mindedly, and change their positions when others are persuasive. They move away from simplistic, right-or-wrong thinking to recognize that they must continually integrate new evidence and ideas as they develop richer understanding and more reasonable conclusions.

Agree and Shake

Select a high-quality solution. The decision should best promote the shared vision and the common interests of the group and organization. It should not be selected because the most powerful favor it.

Implement the solution. The most elegant solution will not be much good unless people are prepared and able to implement it.

Reflect and Learn

Assess implementation and the effects of the solution. Successful solutions are implemented as intended and the consequences are in line with expectations.

Be prepared to recycle through more controversy. A solution that appears satisfactory one week may prove ineffective the next; a solution thought to be easy to implement may turn out not to be. A new round of cooperative conflict can incorporate new information and perspectives.

Discuss the process. Decision makers should give each other feedback and identify the strengths and areas that need improvement to solve future problems more effectively and efficiently.

Hold joint celebrations. Using conflict to make decisions is challenging, but the rewards are considerable. People recognize their abilities and efforts, the quality of the solution, and their confidence in their relationships. They jointly celebrate their success.

Ongoing Improvement

As Eric and others in marketing were discovering, they could not expect to discuss opposing views well without practice. They reflected on how they had used conflict productively. They made realistic plans to strengthen their capabilities.

Like the members of NorTel's marketing group, people involved in cooperative conflict should continually upgrade and refine their abilities because disagreeing constructively without being disagreeable involves complex skills. They must research and collect facts and knowledge as they formulate their positions. They must defend their views in a coherent, reasoned manner by linking facts together into a logical structure that leads to their conclusion.

Controversy requires empassioned arguments as well as rational ones. People should express their positions persuasively and convincingly. But they should restrict their criticism to ideas, not people, and they should not take rejection of their ideas personally.

Eric, Willem, and the marketing people were combining their understanding of cooperative conflict and its procedures to explore important problems and move toward decisions. They were at the same time strengthening their commitment to cooperative conflict, deepening their insights into conflict management, and becoming more confident and skillful. They were learning to use their opposing views to pursue their common goals.

Debates over decisions, though they provoke strong feelings, are focused on differences in ideas about how the group should proceed. But often conflict has more to do with irritations, grievances, and anger that develop as people frustrate each other in their attempts to pursue their own objectives and complete their responsibilities. These conflicts have a raw edge as interests and feelings clash. As the next chapter describes, Eric and the people at NorTel also had to manage these conflicts.

Using Cooperative Conflict in Decision Making

Guides for Action

- Elaborate positions and ideas.
- List facts, information, and theories.
- Ask for clarification.
- Clarify opposing ideas.
- Search for new information.
- Challenge opposing ideas and positions.
- Reaffirm your confidence in those who differ.
- Listen to all ideas.
- Restate opposing arguments that are unclear.
- Identify strengths in opposing arguments.
- Change your mind only when confronted with good evidence.
- Integrate various information and reasoning.
- Create alternative solutions.
- Agree to a solution responsive to several points of view.
- Use a new round of cooperative conflict to develop and refine the solution.

Pitfalls to Avoid

- Assume your position is superior.
- Prove your ideas are right and must be accepted.
- Interpret opposition to your ideas as a personal attack.
- Refuse to admit weaknesses in your position.
- Pretend to listen.
- Ridicule to weaken the others' resolve to disagree.
- Try to win over people to your position through charm and exaggeration.
- See accepting another's ideas as a sign of weakness.

8

Negotiating, Mediating, and Arbitrating

Leave a half dozen of the group, three environmentalists and three industrialists, stranded in a West Virginia holler while the rest of the field trip participants—and the buses—are nowhere to be seen, and they'll find a lot in common.

—Coal Outlook

"Another conflict, another problem," Eric muttered. Nick had just informed Eric that Leslie and Rudy were barely speaking to each other and that their hostility was polluting the department's atmosphere. Eric had sensed that something was amiss.

"Think of it as another opportunity to learn," Nick said dryly, in an attempt to cheer Eric up.

"Sometimes there can be too much of a good thing." Eric was glad he could smile with Nick. "Perhaps I should call them in and have them talk about the problem, let them manage the conflict."

Nick agreed, "Just letting things slide isn't much of an answer. Something needs to be done."

Eric set up a meeting for that afternoon. He had planned to prepare over lunch, but other issues kept him occupied. Soon he was welcoming Leslie and Rudy into his office. Eric liked to have some small talk before the meeting, but he was preoccupied with anxiety about how to begin. He wanted them to manage their conflict cooperatively, but he had no plan. He didn't relish having to improvise.

"Thank you for coming," Eric began. "My idea is that I want you to manage your conflict. Being upset with each other gets in the way of our work, and I would think it even bothers you away from work."

"I don't know if I would call it a conflict," Rudy said. "It's more a matter of what's right and fair."

"But what you consider fair, I don't," Leslie responded.

"Sounds like a conflict to me," Eric said. But Leslie and Rudy were too upset to respond to any levity in Eric's voice. Eric continued. "I don't have a definite plan but I want the two of you to talk to each other and and see if you can resolve your differences cooperatively."

"Like advocacy teams," Leslie said.

"In a way," Eric said. "We don't have teams arguing different opinions, but two people arguing their own. I hope, though, we get the same kind of give-and-take discussions to understand the issues and get an agreement."

Wanting to look reasonable to Eric, Leslie and Rudy both began slowly and factually. Leslie had called upon Prime Communication, Inc. over a six-month period, but when she had gotten additional responsibilities and Rudy had come on board, Leslie introduced Rudy to the company. Rudy then followed through and landed the big contract they had wanted.

"So far, so good," Eric. "Teamwork in action."

"It should be very good, but then Leslie complained about not getting enough of the commission," Rudy said.

"I wasn't being greedy and I wasn't complaining," Leslie said, trying to hold her feelings in check. "I was arguing that it wasn't a fair and reasonable division. Typically in the past we have shared the commission equally."

"Equal may sound nice and may seem natural, but the fact is that I closed the deal," Rudy explained. "Closed deals are what keeps the company going and it was me out there negotiating and satisfying the customer."

"You can't close a deal unless the customer has been found, and that's what I did," Leslie responded. "It's not so much fun making cold calls and getting business leads. You should try it once."

"I have made many cold calls."

Eric interjected, "What we're actually talking about here is a few hundred dollars. That doesn't sound like too big a problem to me."

"Principles are involved, Eric," Leslie said briskly. She didn't like Eric's apparent condescension. "I've seen too many people, often women, whose work wasn't appreciated and who paid the price."

"Well, I appreciate your work." Eric was trying to recover, but he sensed he was getting in the way. He'd let them talk.

"But Rudy goes on and on about how little my efforts at finding this and other customers really count," Leslie said. "He's telling me that he's important and I'm not."

"Calm down, let's stay rational." But Rudy too was angry and fought back. There were charges and countercharges.

Eric began to see how he could apply the idea of cooperative conflict here. "You're both fighting as if you were against each other, as if this were a win–lose situation, when clearly the two of you have cooperative interests."

Leslie and Rudy were irritated at Eric's lecturing. "Each contract gives a total of one-and-a-half percent commission," Rudy said. "The more she gets, the less I get."

"Not everything is win–win," Leslie said curtly.

Leslie and Rudy continued fighting.

Eric could feel that he was getting frustrated both with them for repeating their arguments and with his inability to get them out of the cycle. Then he reminded himself that he could learn. That realization helped him say good naturedly, "Let's see how we can use the tools of cooperative conflict to help us deal with this disagreement."

Both Leslie and Rudy were getting frustrated with their present way of discussing their conflict, and they realized that it was not getting them very far. Yet Eric's idea seemed strange and unrealistic. They were also skeptical because they expected that a comparison with this ideal would make them look ineffectual.

Eric hoped that he could cajole Leslie and Rudy into a learning mode. "First, let's all admit that we haven't been perfect in dealing with this conflict. I haven't and you haven't. Being perfect and being in conflict just don't seem to go together."

"You're right, I've only been close to being perfect," Rudy deadpanned.

"I would have been perfect if Rudy would have let me," Leslie joined in.

"First, have we been discussing this conflict cooperatively or competitively?" Eric asked.

"I would say determinedly," Leslie replied.

"Forcefully," Rudy said.

"I think we can conclude there's been quite a bit of competition of the 'I'm right, you're wrong,' 'I've done more than you have' variety," Eric said trying to sound informative rather than evaluative.

"But how can we fight cooperatively over this issue?" Leslie asked.

"The emphasis should be on how to recognize each other's efforts and how to resolve the conflict so that both people feel fairly treated," Eric said. "It's also important that the resolution helps you both work more effectively together in the future."

"But, Eric, sometimes people have to fight for their rights; you can't expect people to let themselves be walked over," Leslie said.

"I wasn't walking over you," Rudy snapped back.

"But I thought you were trying to walk over me, and I'm not letting that happen," Leslie said.

"Surely when people work together, there's going to be conflict," Eric said. "I wouldn't want you to let people walk over you; sometimes you have to raise a fuss. But in cooperative conflict, you're arguing your case so that you and others can be a more effective team. You're recognizing each other's contributions and learning more about each other."

"Kind of abstract, Eric," Rudy retorted.

"In a way. But in a way, it's very simple," Eric said. "People listen to each other, respect their views, and show that they want a solution good for both."

"But how can we do that here?" Rudy was skeptical.

Eric said, "First, let's remember why we want to manage this conflict. How can the two of you help each other get where you want to go?"

Leslie and Rudy were perplexed by Eric's question and wondered how it was related to the present conflict.

"What comes to my mind first is that to make a deal someone has to find the customer before someone gets to close the deal," Eric said.

"True enough," Rudy said.

"The more customers Leslie finds, the more possibilities Rudy can potentially close," Eric said. "The fact is that we can't do our jobs well without the help of others. How about respect? It has to go two ways. We don't respect people who don't respect us."

"But why do we have all these programs on empowering yourself?" Rudy said.

"And why a compensation system that mostly rewards the one who closes the deal?" Leslie said.

"Some of NorTel's programs get in the way, and this conflict is helping me see that more clearly," Eric said. "But let's stick to this issue. Why don't both of you show you understand the other's arguments. Then let's see if we can brainstorm a resolution both think is reasonable, if not optimal, and that helps the two of you work effectively in the future."

Eric had Leslie and Rudy both rephrase each other's arguments to improve communication. Leslie showed that she understood that Rudy had worked very diligently and creatively and talked to many different people at Prime. Rudy described how Leslie had opened the door and had set positive expectations in place. The conflict took on a more constructive tone as they publicly recognized each other's contributions and discussed how they could be successfully integrated. Leslie felt Rudy appreciated her efforts, but she also found out that Rudy's efforts had been more intensive then she had believed. They developed several options and settled on sixty percent for Rudy and forty percent for Leslie.

"I'll take you both out for a beer after work," Eric said. "Resolving a conflict is as good a reason as any for celebrating. But first, more business. Are there things that we learned?"

"We can manage conflict cooperatively, even over money," Rudy said.

"A little understanding of the other's position goes a long way," Leslie said.

"So does long-term thinking," Rudy said.

"Somehow, though, we had to hash things out. There were things on our minds that needed to be said, then we were more prepared to discuss the conflict effectively," Leslie said.

"Its kind of hard for two people already locked in conflict to see how they need each other and have cooperative interests," Eric said.

"Yes, it's as if the conflict gives you tunnel vision," Rudy said.

"We haven't done a very good job of creating teamwork at NorTel," Eric said. "We've focused so much on the individual, the team has been lost. Any comments on my role trying to help you manage conflict?"

Leslie and Rudy needed time to focus on the question. After nearly a minute, Rudy said, "You didn't tell us to shut up, and that was good."

"It seemed like you were in a hurry, though," Leslie said.

"Yes, I felt I was in a hurry too," Eric said. "I'll have to think about why."

"You expected us to see how we could be cooperative," Rudy said.

"That seemed so clear to me, but not to you," Eric said. "Other comments?"

"I wish I had a clearer understanding of the major steps of negotiating cooperatively," Leslie said.

"We could use some guidance and some training in negotiating," Rudy agreed.

"I have some reading on the phases of negotiations, somewhere," Eric replied. "We could study them together to give us more direction. Thanks for the feedback. See you at five for drinks!"

"How's it going, Eric?" Willem asked as he stopped by Eric's office.

"It's always fun when you're managing conflict," Eric said.

"Are you being consistent or just single-minded?" Willem teased.

"Credible, I prefer to call it." Eric filled him in on yesterday's conflict between Leslie and Rudy. "Overall, I didn't do badly, especially given that I had no action plan. Next time I'll prepare. I got some interesting feedback. They said I was in a hurry."

"You're supposed to be slow?" Willem asked.

"The more I thought about it, the more I saw how when you're outside of the conflict you see things differently than when you're inside it. Time can whiz by when you're arguing, but not when you're watching."

"Maybe that's why I'm so short when my children fight," Willem said. "They don't seem to mind fighting with each other nearly as much as I do."

"Same with us. It was also harder for Rudy and Leslie to see their cooperative goals than for me. But now they want some reading on the steps for cooperative negotiations."

"If they had been fighting cooperatively, they probably wouldn't have needed you. Once in that win–lose mode, it can be hard to see another way."

"Right. Which brings me to another point. It was painfully clear that NorTel and I have not done a very good job of creating a co-operative climate. They were talking about what they had done and why what they had done was more important than the other. They were fighting over one commission, rather than working on how to increase everyone's commission."

"But that would require changing the whole culture at NorTel."

Eric laughed. "Think of it this way. We're not going to run out of work to do in the near future. That's a blessing."

Learning with the Boss

There were significant barriers to learning. Leslie and Rudy were embarrassed by their conflict and their inability to deal with it. They assumed that their angry conflict challenged their reputations as competent professionals and effective employees. They worked hard to hide the conflict from Eric. Perhaps if they thought they could get Eric on their side, they would have involved him. But they knew he would not take sides and feared he would scold them for being petty and unskilled.

They felt trapped. Talking to each other would only escalate the conflict; getting Eric involved could make them look bad. But they felt too strongly to let the conflict go.

When Eric knew that there was a serious conflict, he had confidently relied on his idea of learning to manage conflict cooperatively. He saw the potential gain for all in a direct discussion to deal with the immediate issues and to improve their cooperation. He was so confident that he did not make time to prepare.

Eric was effective, not because he was a highly skilled mediator, but because he created a learning climate. He was far from perfect and did not expect his colleagues to be perfect. What was critical was that they used this conflict to practice, reflect, get feedback, and find ways to improve. Eric wanted Leslie and Rudy to learn to deal with the present and future conflict more cooperatively and effectively. In the future, Eric should be more prepared to mediate successfully. Leslie and Rudy should know and respect each other more, feel more like allies, and be able to work together more effectively. Understanding the conflict in this light helped them see their cooperative goals as well as deal with the immediate conflict issue.

Making Choices

Eric, Nick, Leslie, and Rudy had choices about how they could deal with the conflict. Eric and Nick could have chosen to ignore the conflict and hoped that it would go away. Eric might have listened to both sides and then arbitrated a solution. Leslie and Rudy could have tried to ignore the conflict and let it pass or to strike a quick compromise that got the conflict off the table. While avoiding discussion with each other, they could have turned to friends to form alliances against the other or tried to get Eric to side with them.

Success in managing conflict requires making wise choices. Some minor conflicts should be ignored. Giving in and accommodating on issues unimportant to oneself but important to the other can be very sensible. Other conflicts need to be avoided because people do not have the time, skills, or relationship to make direct negotiations productive.

Understanding cooperative conflict helped Eric make wise choices. He knew that there was an alternative to avoiding or imposing a solution. He concluded that the bonus issue was important enough to be addressed directly and he sensed that cooperative negotiations would be the most useful for promoting the learning and relationship of Leslie and Rudy.

His knowledge of cooperative conflict also clarified the alternative to win–lose, competitive negotiations. Not all conflict negotiations are similar; win–lose negotiations have very different dynamics and consequences from cooperative ones. Studies confirm what most mature managers know: the cooperative approach is much more useful because in an organization and in the world of business what goes around, comes around.

Resolving a conflict by creating a loser not only means that you might have an enemy but that the agreement also has one, because the loser may be preparing to undo your victory and the agreement. Research has not been able to document many organizational situations in which competition is effective. Success in negotiations to resolve conflict comes from knowing what the other wants, knowing what you want, and showing the other how to get what the other really wants while you get what you want.

Phases of Negotiating Conflict Cooperatively

Negotiating conflicts productively requires persistence, skill, and ingenuity as well as knowledge of cooperative conflict. It is essential to understand the phases and procedures of cooperative negotiation

State and Explain Your Position

Negotiation begins when at least one person directly communicates that a conflict needs to be discussed and resolved for mutual benefit. The conflict partners sit down to identify and define the conflict. Each side describes the other's actions and why they have concluded that the other's behavior is interfering or frustrating them. Rather than blaming and evaluating, they share their perceptions and feelings. They recognize that they are not mind readers, but need direct information about each other's feelings and beliefs. Rather than seeing the conflict as a win–lose struggle, they define it as a mutual problem to be solved. No one loses when you solve a mutual problem.

It is critical to focus on needs, feelings, and goals, not just describe one's positions. Cooperative negotiators state why they are proposing their resolution and how it will help them accomplish their needs and strengthen their relationships. They do not assume that incompatible positions and proposals mean that basic goals and interests are in conflict. They seek solutions that further the needs of both persons so that both are committed to resolving the conflict. They see that they have more to gain by a negotiated settlement than by continuing the conflict.

Question and Understand Opposing Views

As the antagonists elaborate on their positions, they listen to learn more about each other's needs, interests, and feelings. They argue to show how their proposals can meet the needs of both persons. They critique opposing solutions and point out their inadequacies. They ask why and why not to look behind positions and proposals. They realize that an advantage of conflict lies in confronting a colleague's or friend's personal, unique perspective and realizing how it is both different and in some ways similar to their own. To create a mutually beneficial agreement, negotiators have to keep in mind their own and the others' perspectives and make an accurate assessment of them.

There are important obstacles to this understanding. We can misjudge the motivation and emotional intensity the other brings to the conflict. We can exaggerate our differences and discount our similarities. Moreover, people in conflict often feel they are not understood and so must repeat their arguments more strongly and loudly. They become intransigent or give up because the other is not listening to them and, therefore, no agreement suitable to them can be arranged.

Putting yourself in the other's shoes by presenting the other's position and reasoning contributes to cooperative negotiations. The other recognizes that you are trying to understand and gives you feedback and additional information to improve your perspective-taking. The other is also more prepared to stop repeating arguments and listen to and consider your views. Then both negotiators are in a better position to develop effective resolutions.

Integrate and Create Options

Through open discussion, negotiators move toward a shared understanding of the conflict that helps them create options that promote mutual goals. But the obstacles to creating solutions are formidable.

Perhaps the most common obstacle is fixation on your original proposal as if it were the only one that could satisfy your requirements. When both people are rigidly committed to their own position and either–or thinking, the issue is often defined in terms of "my way or his way."

Similarly, there is a tendency to assume that the resolution is a fixed pie in which the more one gets, the less the other gets, often accompanied by a short-term perspective. However, a truly fixed pie rarely occurs especially in the long term. Management and labor have competitive interests in terms of wage settlements, but both will benefit from a stronger relationship in which they join forces to reduce costs, improve quality, resolve grievances, and strengthen the firm's security. Generally, the more one gets, the more the other gets.

Premature evaluation also frustrates creating alternatives. Some people are so prepared to pounce on the drawbacks of any new idea that others are reluctant to brainstorm or propose ideas for fear of being shot down.

To create alternatives and overcome these obstacles, negotiators brainstorm and invent as many options as they can. The more ideas, the more likely a good one can be selected. Later negotiations evaluate ideas to the extent they promote mutual benefit.

Negotiators can bundle ideas together and propose package deals. They can reach agreement on several issues simultaneously so that everyone can see that, at least on some issues, their interests have been protected and promoted. Similarly, negotiators can reach agreement on different issues in which a settlement to one issue is linked to a settlement on another.

Agree and Shake

Effective agreements meet the important, legitimate interests of both sides. To the extent possible, such agreements satisfy both sides' mutual needs and reconcile their opposing interests. The negotiators must be able to implement the settlement and committed to sustaining it. No matter how elegant the solution, it cannot solve the conflict unless it is abided by. The agreement should be durable and should help the negotiators put the conflict behind them, get the job done, and prepare for future collaboration. Proceeding successfully through the prior steps is critical for arriving at these agreements.

Ideally, the conflict should be resolved on the basis of objective criteria. The proposals should be evaluated according to standards of fairness, efficiency, community values, and scientific merit. Leslie and Rudy decided to use the standard of equity, in which rewards would be distributed according to how much effort each person had made. Then they evaluated options and made a decision based on the principle of equity. When using a standard is impossible, people can agree to other methods, such as taking turns, drawing lots, or letting someone else decide.

The agreement should indicate that the conflict will end, describe how people are to behave differently in the future, stipulate what should happen if people fail to live up to the agreement, and identify times to discuss the resolution to see if further steps can be taken to improve the relationship. Negotiations are prepared to reopen discussions if the solution proves ineffective. They remember that success in negotiations comes when, to the fullest extent possible, both sides get what they really want.

Reflect and Learn

The protagonists reflect back on their negotiations to learn more about how they approached the conflict and their relationship. By discarding dysfunctional ideas that they should be able to manage their conflict perfectly, they seek to deepen their sensitivities and improve their abilities. They ask for and give each other feedback and the support needed to consider and use the feedback. They celebrate their successes and plan how to change shortcomings. They see how learning to manage conflict binds them cooperatively together.

Negotiating Conflict

Guides for Action

Effective negotiation requires a cooperative context, explaining positions, questioning opposing views, creating options, agreeing and reflecting.

FOSTER COOPERATIVE CONTEXT
- Develop realistic expectations that working together cooperatively requires conflict management.
- Express cooperative expectations.
- Focus on working together to deal with the conflict.
- Avoid finding fault.
- Work for win–win solutions.
- Calculate the gains and losses of continuing the conflict and of resolving it.

STATE AND EXPLAIN YOUR POSITION
- Arrange a time and place to work on conflict.
- Identify ideas and feelings behind positions.
- Be hard on the problem, soft on the person.

QUESTION AND UNDERSTAND OPPOSING VIEWS
- Probe and ask questions.
- Put yourself in the other's shoes.
- Show respect and acceptance as you disagree with the opposing position.
- Follow the golden rule of conflict: use the approach you want others to use.

INTEGRATE AND CREATE OPTIONS
- Define the problem together.
- Be firm in furthering mutual needs, but flexible in how you do so.
- Brainstorm options.

AGREE AND SHAKE
- Agree to an option.
- Reaffirm the agreement.

REFLECT AND LEARN
- Give each other feedback and support.
- Celebrate.

Pitfalls to Avoid

- See the conflict as a problem that must be blamed on someone.
- Assume every conflict is a fight to win.
- Focus only on what you want.
- Portray the situation as "us versus them."
- Assume sole responsibility for resolving the conflict.
- Assume it is the sole responsibility of the other to resolve the conflict.
- Repeat arguments in a louder voice.
- Surprise and overwhelm.
- Hit your protagonist hard, then run to avoid getting hit back.
- Return every slight with a rebuke.

- Pretend to listen.
- Use the other's arguments only to strengthen your position.
- Assume the resolution is either "his way or my way."
- Use either–or, fixed pie thinking.
- Equate success with getting your way.
- Gloat over your victory.

Mediating Conflict

Managers are thrust into the role of mediator of their employees' conflicts. A recent survey by Accountemps, a division of Robert Half International, Inc., found that vice-presidents and personnel directors of one hundred of America's thousand largest corporations exert a great deal of effort to handle problems with conflicting employees. Executives indicated that they spend 9.2 percent of their time attempting to deal with employee conflicts and the difficulties they cause.

Cooperative conflict suggests two powerful, integrated ways that managers and others can help people discuss and manage their differences. The first is to help the conflict partners develop a cooperative context in which they understand that they have important, positively related goals. The second method involves helping them learn cooperative negotiation strategies.

Recognizing Cooperative Goals

Leslie and Rudy emphasized their competitive interests at the expense of their cooperative ones. They disputed over who would win the fight for commissions and who would be seen as more important and valued. Yet they needed each other to work effectively to improve their commissions; they needed each other's respect to feel competent and successful at work. Even their inability to manage the conflict effectively without Eric underlined their cooperative goals. Each needed the other to learn how to manage conflict. Each had much to gain when they both learned to deal with this and other conflicts. Their common need to manage conflict bound them cooperatively together.

In addition to reminding the conflict partners of their cooperative goals, mediators can strengthen the cooperative context by having them assess their goals and how they depend upon each other. The conflict partners break away from discussing the conflict at hand to examine their relationship. This interdependence assessment has four steps.

1. The antagonists list their major objectives and aspirations independently. These can be global ("to feel respected") or specific ("make more commissions"). Learning to manage conflict should be included for both persons.

2. The conflict partners brainstorm how they can help each other reach their goals and how they can get in each other's ways. They should assess their potentials rather than measuring their actual behavior. They should avoid blaming each other for failing to help each other reach goals. List these "failures" as possible ways that they can get in each other's ways.

3. The antagonists negotiate and reach agreements about how they can help each other reach their goals. These agreements should be specific and realistic; they should be fair and mutually agreed upon. Successful follow-up should be recognized and rewarded and violations should be dealt with.

The mediator can guide the antagonists to understand that, though they have incompatible activities, they still have many cooperative goals. They may also see that they put different values on goals so that they can logroll to give each person his or her most important goals. They may formulate superordinate goals that both of them must work together to achieve.

4. The participants reflect upon these activities and discuss what they have learned. They should be able to see concretely how they both will be further ahead by helping each other than by working against each other. They can also discuss the extent to which they have negotiated their agreements for mutual benefit. They have begun to put into practice their agreed-upon procedures and ways to manage their differences. They are jointly reaching agreement about fair and effective ways to work through conflict. They have concrete evidence of their ability to learn to manage their differences cooperatively and productively and the value of this cooperation.

The mediator asks the conflict partners to put aside discussion of the conflict at hand to focus on their cooperative interdependence. However, the exercise is not a way to avoid discussing the conflict issues, but to prepare them for it. They can be asked to discuss how they can use the present conflict to strengthen their cooperative goals and relationship.

Teaching Cooperative Negotiation Strategies

A strong cooperative context facilitates but does not insure productive conflict. The antagonists must still hammer out resolutions. Encouraging and teaching cooperative negotiation strategies can help the conflict partners deal with the specific issues and reduce competitive feelings.

The previous section described the major cooperative skills of elaborating their positions, seeking and demonstrating understanding of the other's views, creating options, and deciding on a settlement. In addition to modeling these strategies and urging protagonists to adopt them, mediators can have the antagonists study and discuss conflict strategies together. This process typically involves the following steps:

1. The conflict partners read and discuss each cooperative conflict strategy.
2. They identify what the behavior "looks like" and what it "sounds like" to make their understanding more concrete and specific.
3. They identify related behaviors that they believe will be useful for them.
4. They discuss and reach an agreement that they should try to use these strategies as they deal with the conflict at hand.
5. They reflect at the end of each session to identify the extent they have and have not used these cooperative conflict strategies. The mediator helps them focus on helping each other learn to use these strategies more appropriately and frequently.

If appropriate time and resources are available, the mediator can provide a training program for the antagonists. For example, they could develop a clear understanding of the need to develop cooperative conflict skills and their nature, observe a behavioral model of cooperative conflict, discuss the effectiveness and uses of this approach, practice role playing cooperative negotiations, and receive feedback and support to continue to learn.

Reflect and Learn

Eric, like most mediators, wanted to empower his employees by helping them develop the skills to deal with future conflicts. In addition to the pressure for an agreement to the immediate issue, the lack of a shared framework frustrates this learning. The theory of cooperative conflict gives mediators and conflict partners a common understanding. Then they have a shared ideal for how they are trying to discuss their differences and can give each other feedback and support to improve how they deal with present and future conflicts.

Arbitrate

Eric could have chosen to arbitrate the dispute between Leslie and Rudy by listening to both sides and then making a decision to resolve the conflict. Although, as Eric saw, direct negotiations usually are considered more fair and result in more learning, arbitration can be very useful for resolving conflict. Informal arbitration is very popular within organizations, but is often carried out in abbreviated, ineffective ways.

An arbitrator takes an unbiased position to become familiar with the problem, the opposing positions, and the evidence. Then the arbitrator renders a judgment about how the conflict should be resolved. The process includes:

1. The conflict partners both agree that they will abide by the arbitrator's decision after they have had a chance to present their sides of the conflict.
2. Both sides submit their positions and how they want the conflict to be resolved to focus the discussion and decision.
3. Both present their positions and supporting evidence without interruption. Each side has an equal opportunity to present its case.
4. Each side refutes and provides evidence to counter the other side's arguments and evidence. They try to persuade the arbitrator through facts and logic.
5. Both sides make a closing statement.
6. The arbitrator announces the decision and its rationale.

Ideally, arbitration is voluntary. Two companies agree to ask an arbitrator to decide a breach of contract and abide by the decision. Two countries agree to let the World Court resolve a territorial dispute. But within organizations, employees usually assume that they must submit to informal arbitration by their boss. The traditional hierarchy gives managers the authority and responsibility to settle disputes and insure smooth coordination. Indeed, passing a conflict up the hierarchy is, after avoidance, perhaps the most popular way to deal with conflict in organizations.

But managers are seldom prepared to arbitrate effectively. They are not without prejudice: rather, they bring strong attitudes and biases toward the conflict partners and their conflict. Feeling they do not have the time to proceed through the steps of arbitration thoroughly, managers often short-cut the process by making a decision after listening to one side. They dismiss preparing positions as time wasted in brooding and view refuting arguments as squabbling.

Employees also are often unprepared. They are angry but are unsure why, and they are unclear about what the resolution should be. Even when they know, they might be embarrassed to write and discuss their position with the manager. They remain fixed on their position, and when that is not completely accepted, they feel they have lost, blame the manager as unfair, and withdraw from work.

Arbitration is overused and negotiation is underused in organizations. Although both can result in poor solutions and weakened relationships, cooperative negotiation provides more face-to-face opportunities to present and understand each other's point of view, to create new alternatives, and to reach an agreement that people believe is fair and effective. Negotiations and mediation also provide more opportunities to practice and learn the complex skills of conflict management.

Negotiation involves, but is much more than, rational problem solving. As dealing with differences invoke strong needs, goals, and fears, managing conflict is an emotional as well as intellectual challenge. We are often ineffective in dealing with feelings and try to cope by striving for the unrealistic, misguided ideal of being unemotional in conflict. The next chapter explores how we can manage the perplexing feeling of anger so that it contributes to productive relationships.

Mediating Conflict

Guides for Action

ESTABLISH A COOPERATIVE CONTEXT

- Promote a climate in which conflicts are addressed.
- Develop a strong, cooperative team organization.
- Have antagonists assess their cooperative and competitive goals.
- Brainstorm ways they can help each other accomplish goals.
- Decide how they can promote mutual goals.

DEVELOP OPEN DISCUSSION

- Identify cooperative negotiation skills as ideals to strive for.
- Encourage stating position, exploring the opposing position, creating solutions, and reaching an agreement.
- Practice cooperative conflict skills.

REFLECT AND LEARN

- Have antagonists reflect on their negotiation to identify areas of strength and areas for improvement.
- Ask for feedback on the effects of your mediation.

Pitfalls to Avoid

- Convey you are too busy to bother with petty squabbling.
- Try to discover who is to blame for the conflict.
- Assume the antagonists see their cooperative goals when you do.
- Assume the antagonists should be skillful negotiators.
- Push for the resolution first proposed.
- Try to resolve conflict as quickly as possible.
- Get through the conflict without reflecting and learning.

9

Managing Anger at Home and Work

I was angry with my friend:
I told my wrath, my wrath did end.
I was anger with my foe:
I told it not, my wrath did grow.

—William Blake

"I can't figure you out. Why did you marry someone like me if you wanted Miss Goody Two Shoes," Carol said sharply and angrily.

"Don't get all upset over nothing." Eric prided himself on the self-control he had developed over the years of dealing with his impetuous wife. "I just don't think that it's very good for you or for us to have the place so messy and the kids going off to school dirty." He now wished he hadn't brought these matters up, but he had. Perhaps he was tired of protecting his wife. Perhaps it was his conflict management activities at work. But now that he had begun, he would make his points.

"Thank you for being so helpful," Carol said sarcastically. She could feel her battling juices flowing, but it was hard to do battle with Eric. Still, he had started the fight, and she felt no responsibility to end it. She had things to get off her chest.

"Just trying to make things a little better for everyone," Eric said with a laugh.

"Don't try to joke about it. It's not funny."

"Okay, I won't joke. But there's no reason why those kids can't go to school with clean clothes and why we can't eat breakfast on a clean table." He would not joke—he recalled Willem's feedback about not joking in conflict—but he felt hurt by her harshness.

"See that rag, hubby? You use if it's so important to clean the table."

Eric was dumbfounded by his wife's fury. "I do my fair share of work around the house. Your job is to keep the place clean. It's not too much to ask."

"There's more to life than cleaning house."

"But it's all part of having a family. You have two wonderful children and a husband who provides for you. I don't feel sorry for you."

"You're so pompous. You spend all day cleaning and see how you like it."

"Carol, most jobs are much more boring than raising children. What has that women's group been pumping into your head?"

"It hasn't pumped anything into me. It's helped me think about myself and my relationships more clearly."

"I hadn't noticed." As soon as he said it, he wished he hadn't.

"You're so much into your own world, it would take a sledge hammer to get you to notice. You're on this big managing conflict kick. I haven't noticed either. You're the same chicken, the same conflict avoider you've always been."

Eric dreaded these times. He could feel the desire to lash out at his wife and inflict harm. He had a deep sense of failure. He had put so much energy into his relationship with his wife, yet it had come to this. "You're the one who's chicken. If I say anything, you go crazy."

"Living with you would drive anyone crazy."

Eric was torn. He didn't want to give up the fight, but he didn't want it to get worse either. "I have to go to work. Not everyone can sit at home and feel sorry for themselves."

"Is the chicken leaving for work? Perhaps you can boss those people around there."

Eric was relieved to be alone in his car and in a few minutes he regreted that he had allowed himself to blow up. Now he would spend the day both waiting to patch things up at home and dreading having to go home. He had other things to do at work than worry about fights with his wife.

Halfway through the morning, he called Anthony to have lunch together. He'd have to drive across town to see Anthony, but it would be worth it.

"Must be something important to make you drive way over here for lunch," Anthony said as they sat down. "Restaurants got salmonella on the rich part of town? Or you've been fighting with your wife?"

"How did you know? Have you been looking through breakfast nook windows again?"

"Hey, I fight with my girlfriend, you fight with your wife. It's always a good guess."

Eric felt better already. He summarized the morning's events and gave some specifics.

"She's still not used to how sensitive you are," Anthony interjected. "Either that or she was really angry."

"She was angry." Eric was taken back by Anthony's comment.

"I've had some good talks with Carol the last few months," Anthony said. "I think she's got some things on her mind. To her credit, she's been thinking about the meaning of life and her purpose. It's natural when you're questioning like that to be a little edgy, to be both confident and unconfident. She's an interesting, strong woman, and reasonable, too."

Driving back to the office, Eric felt lucky to have Anthony as a friend. He was on Eric's side, but also on Carol's side. Eric decided he would try to keep his anger and sensitivity under control. He would really listen to his wife. Perhaps he could learn how to manage angry conflict, too, and learn more about Carol, himself, and their relationship.

Eric was eager to get home and make amends. Carol welcomed his smile and embrace, but he could tell that she was in feisty mood. The crisis was not over.

Typically, he would let things slide and say he was sorry for getting upset in the hope of putting the conflict behind and avoiding another angry outburst. But he had decided to try to make something good come out of the conflict. After the kids fell asleep would be the time to reopen the discussion. Though he felt hesitant and ambiguous, he was determined to carry out his simple plan of listening.

"Carol, I hope we can talk about some of the things that were mentioned this morning. I'm going to try to listen to you."

"Without defending yourself?"

He could feel himself being pushed to say something like, "Is that so hard to believe?" but he thought that kind of response would get in the way. So he simply answered, "Without defending myself."

"I've thought about this morning myself and talked it over with Lorraine. What gets me so angry is that I try so hard to please the family and at the same time try to create some kind of career for myself and you're screaming about a little dirt and dust. Big deal."

Eric held back the impulse to critically ask her to explain her notion of a career. She hadn't worked outside the house since their marriage. "I agree that a clean shirt is not that important next to a question like what you are to do with your life. Tell me more about your thoughts on a career."

Carol explained she felt the years had slipped by. She was in her late thirties, and the children were nearly teenagers. She was tired of telling people that she was only a housewife. Yet she had very little idea of what she was going to do for the next decades.

Eric nodded and tried to sound consultative. "To me, raising children and managing a household is a good career, lots more important and challenging than most jobs out there in the so-called real world."

"There you go again. You're telling me what to do!"

"I'm not telling you what to do."

"Yes you are, and you said you were going to listen to me."

Eric felt trapped. He could only think of things to say that would fuel the flame, and he knew there was enough heat already.

"We always have to do it your way," Carol accused. "You don't want me to work, so I don't work. You don't want to talk about this, so we don't. Your way, your way, your way, and I'm sick of it."

Eric's head was spinning, and he wondered why this could be happening to him. Why should such a reasonable and generous husband and father be so accused? "I'm not telling you what to do, and I've always been ready to talk about things."

"What a laugh that is! I'd be in stitches if it wasn't so far from reality. You're so busy with your precious work and keeping your precious body in shape that you don't have time for the rest of us. And then you have the nerve to read your spy novels when you're home, and heaven help anyone who disturbs you."

"I've been very good to you and the kids."

"Sure. You buy us off. You let me spend money, and you're forever giving in and giving things to the kids. If they fight over something, you buy two. The reason we bought this house is because you were tired of having them fight over how late to turn the light off in their bedroom. But do you ever talk to them about a serious problem and tell them 'no?' Forget it—no way."

"Do you want me to be a miserly father like my dad? No, thank you."

"A different era altogether. But you're like your father in that you don't talk about problems."

Eric saw some truth in what Carol was saying. "We Kessels are a rather taciturn lot."

"Don't blame your father. He never told you you had to be like him." Carol smiled slightly. "I guess I've been a little rough, and you've been pretty good about listening."

Eric welcomed the release of pressure and smiled, yet he wanted to pursue the issue. "You really think we've been avoiding discussing problems and that's because I wanted to?"

"Yes. Nearly everyone in our woman's group is in the same boat. Some husbands huff and puff, yell and swear, and some are quiet and meek, but they all avoid discussing problems directly. To be frank, I think I've helped you."

"Perhaps we should sleep on that. Can we talk again tomorrow?"

"Tomorrow night, the next night, and the next night. I'll be here."

Eric and Carol talked the next night and for several nights after that. Eric was committed to learning, and his willingness to consider that he had been avoiding conflict made Carol more relaxed and less angry. They decided that they had to discuss Carol's career more. The children required less time, but still had many psychological and social needs that demanded attention. They would also read and attend classes on communication and managing conflict in the family.

They saw more clearly that they had both assumed they would relate to each other and raise the family much as their parents had. The generations were similar in not managing conflict within the family. But whereas their parents had been strict, Carol and Eric gave in to their children. They shouldn't blame their parents. They would have to find ways of living together that fit them and their time.

Confronting Our Destructive Attitudes Toward Anger

Carol vented her angry at Eric and Eric at Carol. Although he suffered and even wanted revenge, Eric exercised self-discipline that helped both of them make their discussion constructive. They were beginning to channel their anger to help them negotiate their differences and solve problems. They were also confronting common, but destructive, attitudes toward anger.

Anger-Negative Values

Much is blamed on anger. We blame anger for making us say things that hurt others and make conflicts "personal." A manager's angry outburst fuels suspicion and challenges his image as an outgoing, approachable person or as a firm-handed, respected disciplinarian. Angry employees are fired; highly angry people are locked up in prisons and institutions. Anger is equated with explosive, uncontrolled conflict and is considered contrary to good relationships, cooperation, and rational problem solving.

Our prejudices against anger lead us to avoid dealing directly with important issues. We waste our energy by holding anger inside. We feel more irritable and depressed and develop ulcers and other stress-related illnesses. We blame ourselves for getting angry and blame others because the conflict remains frustrating. We give anger the power to destroy and doubt we can do much but try again to suppress our feelings.

Unmanaged anger can result in shouting and cursing, headaches and heart attacks, broken furniture and broken lives, threats and violence. But anger itself does not cause havoc; our unrealistic attitudes and inabilities to express it properly give anger its destructive power.

Getting Angry

Our prejudices extend to defining anger and what lies behind it. We assume we get angry because someone did something to us

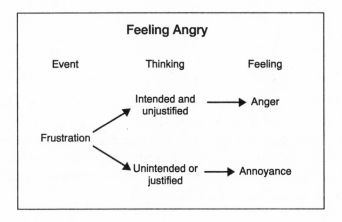

that weakened our rational thinking, overcame our self-control, and made us angry. Intense anger seems to strike quickly and as quickly subside. Although we believe others cause and provoke our anger, we decide when to get angry based on our perceptions and thinking.

Carol was angry with Eric because she thought he was intentionally frustrating her attempts to be valued and her long-range plans to develop a career. Anger is based on the perception of an avoidable, unjustified frustration. Carol thought Eric deliberately affronted her and avoided talking about issues she wanted to discuss. Eric got angry because he thought Carol had attacked him to avoid facing her own shortcomings.

People who obstruct us with sufficient reason or without intention or knowledge may annoy, but not anger. We are angry when a boss leaves us extra work because he wants to lie on the beach, but are only inconvenienced and may be glad to help when he has to attend to a sick child. Anger is particularly intense when others are thought to be obstructing our self-esteem and social status.

The Value of Anger

A close look at anger dispels the popular belief that anger is an antisocial force. People who kept a daily diary of their feelings of anger and irritation were found to get angry with other people, seldom with inanimate objects. Most often they got angry with loved ones and people they liked, and sometimes with acquaintances. The least likely target of anger was people they did not like.

Anger is part of the richness and complexity of managing conflict. If managed well, anger contributes significantly to cooperative conflict. It promotes confronting problems and elaborating positions, emphasizes a cooperative context, and fuels ongoing improvement.

Anger's Value

Dealing with Conflict

Sends a signal. Anger is a signal that helps people scan and understand what is happening. Discovering they are angry leads them to search for frustrating and unproductive events and conflicts.

Focuses and motivates. Anger disrupts ongoing behavior by making people agitated and by interfering with normal information processing. Angry people want to correct perceived injustice and counter aggression. Expressing anger gets the attention of others and motivates them to deal with the conflict.

Builds confidence. Angry people have a sense of virtue and self-righteousness in the face of the opposition of others. They are willing to speak out and challenge people.

Releases frustration and criticism. Angry people often feel released to express suppressed frustration and negative feedback. This communication identifies problems that can be dealt with and solved to strengthen the relationship.

Moves people to action. Anger transforms internal anxiety into external conflict. Anger overcomes fears and inhibitions and helps people take action, defend themselves, and feel more powerful.

Cooperative Relationship

Reaffirms dependence. People usually get angry with people who are important to them. Anger is fundamentally a sign of dependence and of valuing other people.

Strengthens collaboration. Skillful anger communicates that people want to work out difficulties and problems in order to improve how they work together with others to get things done.

Learn and Reflect

Energizes. Anger mobilizes and increases the vigor of actions. People can use this energy to deal with problems, achieve their goals, and strengthen their abilities.

Increases self-awareness. By examining what makes us angry, we learn more about ourselves, our commitments, and our values.

Develops awareness of others. By learning what makes our friends and colleagues angry, we know more about their commitments, values, and priorities.

Conflict without anger can be shallow and unproductive. People who do not express their anger may be unaware of frustrations and blame themselves for being demoralized and depressed. When people do not express anger, others are uncertain if the problems are important and worthy of their attention. Nor do they understand the grievances or feel compelled to act.

Suppressed anger often gets displaced as aggression toward innocent friends and can erupt into violence. Repressing anger gives us headaches, high blood pressure, and ulcers. Repeated failure to express anger tells our colleagues and friends that we are disinterested and uninvolved. It can also convince us that we are powerless to deal with our difficulties.

Making Choices

Eric was controlled by anger. If Carol got angry with him, he would get angry back. Then he would suppress his feelings or strike back if sufficiently provoked. Lashing back created much more fire and energy, but left him feeling more dejected and alienated from Carol. Suppressing his feelings made him feel more powerless and made Carol more pessimistic that she could get him to deal with issues important to her.

Eric was determined to reflect upon his and Carol's anger and to make the conflict useful. He was learning to make choices about how to respond to someone's anger, when to get angry, and how to express it.

Eric realized that responding to Carol's anger by getting angry and to ridiculing her was counterproductive. With Anthony's assis-

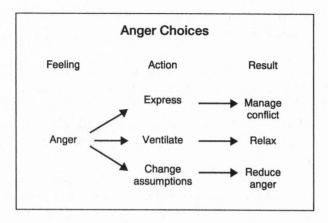

tance, he began to see that how he considered and thought about Carol's anger greatly affected his response. He usually saw Carol's anger as an attempt to avoid her responsibilities as a mother, and therefore he got angry. However, as he began to see that Carol was venting legitimate frustrations over her life goals, Eric felt compassionate and concerned.

Research documents that we have choices about how we deal with and express our anger. Indeed, people find it easier to control what they do than to control how they think about angry situations. People verbally lash out and punish, but they also talk to the person without hostility, talk to others to get their perspective, ventilate, gossip to get back, and take their anger out on others. People are by no means programmed to deal with anger in one way; they have options.

We can control anger, rather than allowing anger to control us. Other people do not make us angry—our conclusions that their actions were frustrating, intentional, and illegitimate create anger. By changing our thinking we can change our emotions. Nor must we respond to anger in one way. Unfortunately, many people are unaware of how they choose to be angry and deal with their anger.

Expressing Anger to Manage Conflict

Carol used her anger to focus needed attention on her perspective and life goals. Her direct, forceful expression helped Eric see shortcomings in his management of conflict at home and find a new determination to change. Yet the way she expressed her anger also made it difficult for Eric to consider her perspective open-mindedly.

Eric thought Carol was too demanding, and he was tempted to respond first with a counterattack and later with avoidance. Yet this way of handling anger can be devastating. Both of them could have ended up thinking about how to get even and take revenge. As a consequence, their frustrations would grow and their relationship deteriorate.

But Eric and Carol were able to use their anger to move toward solving problems and negotiating their differences. They were learning more about each person's needs so that they could negotiate an agreement that gave both of them what they really wanted. They were coming to accept anger as natural and normal, not something they blamed on the other or themselves.

The procedures that help to express anger to make conflict more cooperative and productive can be divided into six categories, similar to those for managing conflict.

1. Establish a cooperative context:

- Show commitment to the relationship. Angry persons depend upon and usually like the people they are angry with. People expect help from friends who have proved trustworthy and are angry when it is not forthcoming. Expressing positive feelings toward the other as a person while angry at his or her behavior can convey a cooperative conflict.
- Check self-righteousness. People can feel powerful, superior, and correct. Angry people can play, "Now I've got you and you'll pay." But anger should be used to get to the heart of the matter, solve problems, and strengthen relationships, not for showing off moral superiority.
- Watch for impulsiveness. Anger agitates people and leads them to say things they regret later.
- Avoid provoking anger. Expressing anger through unfair, insinuating remarks ("I can't believe someone can be as stupid as you!") can make your target angry, too. Such situations can quickly deteriorate.

2. State and explain your position:

- Describe feelings. Clear identification of feelings and what led to them ("I'm upset because you told me to complete the work overnight when you know that my daughter has a piano recital") helps the other person focus on the concrete situation and believe that he or she can do something about it. Abstract judgments ("You're an insensitive, egocentric slavedriver") are coercive and demoralizing.
- Be specific. People find being the target of anger stressful and anxiety provoking. They fear insults and rejection. The more specific the angry person can be, the less threatening and less of an attack on self-esteem that anger is. Knowing what angered the other can give the target of the anger concrete ways to make amends.
- Take responsibility for anger. People should let the target know that they are angry and point out the reasoning that made them feel unjustly frustrated.
- Be consistent. Verbal and nonverbal messages should both express anger. A serious expression, cold tone of voice, direct eye contact, and stiff posture reinforce expressing anger verbally. Smiling and verbally expressing anger causes confusion.

3. Question and understand opposing views:

- Check assumptions. No matter how convinced you are that another has deliberately interfered and wanted to harm you, you may be mistaken. You can ask questions and probe. It may be that the other person had no intention and was unaware that you were frustrated. The incident may dissolve into a misunderstanding and annoyance.
- Be sensitive. People typically underestimate the impact their anger has on others. Targets of anger often feel defensive, anxious, and worried. It is not usually necessary to repeat one's anger to get people's attention.
- Check reactions. Asking the target of the anger how he or she is responding to anger is usually safer than relying on your perceptions. In the heat of the battle, our own fears and frustrations interfere with our assessment of others' feelings and intentions.

4. Integrate and create options:

- Move to constructive conflict management. Feeling affronted, personally attacked, and self-righteous should not sidetrack you from solving the underlying problems.
- Ask for help in developing solutions. Targets of anger can be very interested in finding a solution that restores the relationship, but often assume that their only options are to give in or to counterattack.

5. Agree and shake:

- Put anger behind. Agree to a solution that reduces anger for you and your conflict partner and makes it less likely that both of you will feel angry and estranged.
- Make expression cathartic. Anger generates energy. Telling people releases that energy rather than trying to submerge it. Anger is a feeling to get over with, not to hang on to.

6. Reflect and learn:

- Celebrate joint success. Anger tests people's skills and their relationships. Be sure to celebrate the mutual achievement of expressing and responding to anger successfully.
- Reflect on the experience. Expressing and responding to anger successfully are challenging, complex skills that require ongoing learning.

Managing Anger

Guides for Action

- Recognize when you are angry.
- Decide how to express it.
- Be sensitive that friends and colleagues often find being the target of anger stressful.
- Develop the skills to express anger, ventilate and change assumptions.
- Form strong relationships that allow direct discussions of anger and conflict.
- Focus on the problem at hand.
- Congratulate yourselves when you both express and respond to anger well.
- Appreciate that it will take practice for you and your colleagues to make anger positive.

Pitfalls to Avoid

- Let others push your button.
- Expect others to be perfect.
- Expect yourself to be perfect.
- Blame others.
- Blame yourself for feeling angry.
- Take every disagreement as an attack on your competence.
- Revel in self-righteousness.
- Express your anger through sarcasm, being unhelpful, and other indirect methods.
- Insult others to express your strong feelings.
- Assume you should get angry when another is angry with you.

Expressing Anger

Guides for Action

- Describe feelings and what lies behind them.
- Specify the concrete actions the other took that led to your anger.
- Own and take responsibility for anger by showing how you interpreted the situation and drew conclusions.
- Consistently convey verbal and nonverbal anger.
- Show commitment to the relationship and affection for the person.
- Check assumptions about your conclusion that the other acted deliberately and intentionally.
- Be sensitive that you might be tougher and more stressful to the other than you want.
- Check reactions to understand how the other is responding to your anger.
- Move to constructive conflict management and effective resolution.
- Ask the other to help develop solutions.
- Make expression cathartic so that you release the energy of your anger and get over feeling angry.
- Celebrate your success in expressing anger and the other's in responding to it.
- Reflect on the experience to improve the complex skills of expressing and responding to anger.

Pitfalls to Avoid

- Gossip about another's meanness to colleagues.
- Complain about the other in abstract, general terms.
- Condemn the other as if you were completely faultless.
- Say whatever comes to mind that will make your message powerful.
- Get the other angry so that you are not the only one acting harshly.

Ventilating

Through talking with Anthony, Eric released some of the energy behind his anger toward Carol and took perspective. Eric found that running helped him keep his angry feelings at manageable levels. Sometimes ventilating is necessary because directly expressing anger toward the person is not possible or desirable. It may not be wise or practical to confront an overly stressed family member, an intolerable boss, a new customer, or a preoccupied colleague.

Techniques for releasing anger include exercise. Vigorous and active activities such as running, swimming, racket sports, and fast walking are useful. Shouting, screaming, crying, throwing things, and punching pillows release energy.

Like Eric, you can also ventilate by talking to others. People spend a great deal of time confiding, complaining, and gossiping. When others listen, such talk helps reduce the power of anger. When they encourage revenge, talking with others intensifies anger.

Another productive approach is to resolve the situation in your mind. After deciding that you do not want to be so angry, find ways to view the frustration as something you can live with. Give up telling yourself that the other should act more fairly and justly. Focus on relaxation rather than revenge.

Reducing Chronic Anger

Overly hostile people give anger a bad name and sustain our anger-negative values. They are "hostile," "difficult," "high strung," "no fun" people who are "always complaining" and "never satisfied." They continually exasperate others and ruin their own mood. Where others see mistakes and slights that can be forgiven and forgotten, they see transgressions and injustices that must be condemned and corrected. They are unskilled in managing their anger. More fundamentally, they are not learning from getting angry, but blame their anger on others and themselves.

Blaming versus Learning

Blaming is a common, but destructive, manifestation of anger. Blame-oriented people believe they ought to get their way and that any result short of this is a catastrophe. No shortcoming is too slight not to mull over. All mistakes become grievous errors; small events, major disasters. If their boss cancels a lunch meeting, they take it as if they had just been fired.

Such people are perfectionists in that they expect people to be able to live up to absolute standards. They have not learned that good enough is often the best that can be expected and more than adequate.

Blaming also develops from suspicion. Blamers suspect that they have not gotten their way and things are not perfect because people are mean-spirited and have acted competitively and intentionally. Even though they protected themselves, their enemies still manage to wreak havoc.

Blame can be directed at oneself as well as others. Self-blamers expect themselves to be able to perform perfectly, hold themselves responsible, and believe that they should be punished when they perform imperfectly. They attack themselves as unworthy persons. They hope that such suffering will make them a more successful and worthy person.

But blaming and suffering do not deepen confidence and competence—learning does. Learning is based on the assumption that mistakes and shortcomings are not catastrophes, but can be very useful for keeping us in touch with our friends and colleagues, making our expectations more realistic, and improving our abilities. Rather than being perfectionistic, learning-oriented people consider shortcomings and shortfalls as natural and inevitable. There is no reason to assume that others are mischievous. Indeed, they are united with their conflict partners in an effort to make use of mistakes and problems to strengthen cooperative relationships and promote mutual competence.

Blame-oriented people assume the best that can be done is to try to forget and hope that they are luckier in the future. Learning-oriented people forgive others and themselves and use their experiences to become more realistic, optimistic, and effective.

Moving from Blaming to Learning

Managing conflict cooperatively is a central way to overcome a blame orientation. It gives people experience in confronting troubles and mistakes together to strengthen relationships and improve abilities. However, blame-oriented assumptions frustrate such experiences because people are too suspicious and disheartened to deal directly and cooperatively with conflicts.

Conflictful discussions focused on the destructiveness of blaming assumptions can help people develop learning assumptions. Through discussions with colleagues and friends, blame-oriented people can recognize their troubling, irrational assumptions and replace them with learning-focused, rational ones. They engage in an internal debate to convince themselves to adopt more useful assumptions.

Common troubling assumptions are:

- I am a good person, so everyone should like and respect me all the time.
- Every person who gets angry at me has acted unjustly and unfairly.
- Every criticism is designed to make me look foolish and weak, and my self-respect and social respect demand that I counterattack.
- God gave me the right to do what I want without interruption and anyone who infringes on this right is wrong and no longer a worthy person.

People should examine their own assumptions, realize how they affect their interpretations of situations, identify assumptions that lead to overly angry feelings, dispose of these assumptions, and replace them with more reasonable ones, including:

- Although I am a good person, I will do things that will upset and frustrate others.

- People who get angry with me often value me and our relationship and want to deal with problems and make our relationship stronger.
- Criticism and negative feedback can help me become more self-aware and stimulate improvements in my competence and skills.
- It would be nice if I were left in peace to do what I want, but I can easily live with nuisances.

Anger is natural and inevitable, but some people find themselves angry when they do not want to be or are too frequently angry. Every time a mistake is made, they are angry and blaming. Every time someone else is angry, they counterattack. By focusing less on who can be blamed and more on what can be learned, anger can be more productive.

Reducing Chronic Anger

Guides for Action

- Appreciate the potentially valuable lessons from anger.
- Use mistakes and slights to learn.
- Recognize that you and others can do well enough without being perfect.
- Trust that most people want to be caring, helpful family members and colleagues.
- Forgive others and yourself.
- Confront unrealistic, blame-oriented assumptions.
- Adopt constructive, learning-oriented assumptions.

Pitfalls to Avoid

- Assume every slight is a painful wound.
- Equate not getting what you want with catastrophe.
- See every mistake and slip as a transgression that must be corrected immediately.
- Attack someone for your getting angry.
- Attack yourself for getting angry.
- Try to be and have things perfect.
- Suspect people's motives unless you have incontestable evidence that people can be trusted.

- Assume any attempt to change yourself is an admission of failure.
- Never forgive.

Responding to Provocation

Eric felt that Carol was provoking him. She was angry at him and vented that anger and pent up frustration. Like many other people, she did not always follow this chapter's guides for expressing anger! In addition to expressing anger directly, venting feelings, and modifying our thinking and changing assumptions, there are other points to keep in mind when dealing with provocations.

First, before the provocation, develop realistic expectations. We can remind ourselves of the pressures and limitations on the other. People have different, but not necessarily inferior, ways of expressing themselves. It is not realistic to expect them always to communicate politely, calmly, and reasonably. Nor does it make sense to get angry just because the other person is. We should have reasonable assumptions and bring a learning, not a blaming, orientation to provocations.

Second, during the provocation, experience the outburst and work to cope with it. We should not take criticisms too personally, but should remind ourselves that people exaggerate and do not mean for their statements to be taken literally. An angry person lets off steam, and as soon as he or she has released that frustration, we can begin to solve the problem. There is no need to doubt yourself, even if your colleague does. Take the long view and avoid a counterattack that would continue the negative conflict and cause everyone to lose.

Finally, after the outburst, celebrate your strength and success in keeping cool and in charge of yourselves and the situation. Share your experiences with friends and colleagues and develop ways to be better prepared to respond to future provocations.

Responding to Angry Provocation

Guides for Action

- Expect angry people to exaggerate.
- Recognize the other's frustrations and pressures.

- Use the provocation to develop your abilities.
- Allow the other to let off steam.
- Begin to problem solve when the anger is at moderate levels.
- Congratulate yourself on turning an outburst into an opportunity to find solutions.
- Share successes with partners.

Pitfalls to Avoid

- Take every word literally.
- Denounce the most extreme statements and ignore more moderate ones.
- Doubt yourself because the other does.
- Attack because you have been attacked.
- Forget the experience without learning from it.

Becoming Anger-Positive

Attitudes toward anger place our biases against conflict in bold relief. Of all our prejudices toward conflict, those against anger are the strongest and most destructive. But anger cannot be shoved aside and driven away. The only realistic ideal is to find constructive outlets that use our anger to help us negotiate our important differences and solve vital problems.

Anger is a test of conflict. If managed well, anger contributes to the productive power of conflict. Unmanaged anger intensifies conflict and feeds more anger and disruption. Unfortunately, how anger is handled often interferes with people feeling that their conflict is cooperative because anger has been allowed to degenerate into a win–lose, "I'm right, you're wrong" competitive struggle. But the skilled expression of anger can reassert people's cooperative reliance on each other and their need to discuss their conflicts.

Eric was learning that anger could be useful for learning to manage conflict cooperatively and for learning more about himself and his partners. He had better insight into his own sensitivity and into what led him to feel competitive and angry. He was more focused on how he could change some of his assumptions so that he would not needlessly get angry and upset. He was also beginning to appreciate the value of the direct expression of anger and the need to ventilate and talk about anger with friends.

Eric was challenged to translate his insights about anger to the workplace. He saw that the popular notion that conflicts in organizations should be limited to disagreements over impersonal tasks was unrealistic and unworkable. The marketing people in the advocacy team had strong feelings as they argued their positions with conviction. Leslie and Rudy felt angry and annoyed at each other and at Eric as they tried to negotiate their differences.

These insights helped him to see how the roles and values of his professional and organizational life reinforced prejudices against anger and frustrated a more useful attitude toward anger. He became more committed to making his company more conflict-positive. The next section describes how organizations can move toward adopting cooperative conflict and positive anger.

PART FOUR

Reaching Out

[T]he weakest link in the chain of cooperative effort is the will to collaborate....our hands are held back again and again in doing things known to be technically or commercially feasible, because of the fear that the human being with whom we work will not sufficiently collaborate with us or with each other.

—*Chester Barnard*

When our conflict partners understand and apply the idea of cooperative conflict, we are more able to deal with our conflicts. By encouraging them to manage conflict cooperatively, we sharpen our conflict abilities. Chapter 10 shows how cooperative conflict can help focus an organization on developing its conflict capabilities. Chapter 11 describes the use of teams to support the ongoing development of individuals. Chapter 12 suggests how managing conflict cooperatively offers a comprehensive way to promote individual learning and organizational change and to create an integrated environment for working and living together.

10

Changing an Organization

When two men in business always agree, one of them is unnecessary.
—*William Wrigley, Jr.*

"Wendy and I both agree there are advantages to managing conflict, and—perhaps—NorTel should put more effort into it. But, Eric, you must also see that change like this takes time," Hugh said. Wendy, who listened quietly, agreed with Hugh, but thought it best that Eric be dealt with by his boss.

Eric could see Hugh's point, and he did not blame Hugh or Wendy, yet he was frustrated. He was fighting with the NorTel executives, but they were not there. "This discussion just shows why we need a cooperative conflict program. Here I am debating with you, but you tell me that the executives are not ready for a managing conflict program. Wouldn't it be more fruitful if we all debated this together?"

"Eric, you know that's not how we do things at NorTel," Hugh said. He appreciated Eric's conviction, but he was annoyed that Eric was so insistent. What was he supposed to do? He had given Eric his best advice: The executives were not prepared even to hear about a program to make NorTel a conflict-positive organization.

Eric saw Hugh's annoyance and knew that he did not want to push him too far. "I know I'm being strong-minded, perhaps even pig-headed, and I don't want to go around and around like a broken record, but it's so clear to me. Don't the executives talk about how they want a bottom-up management style where people come up with ideas for change?" Eric was not ready to give up. "Here's a bottom-up idea, and it's an idea that can make bottom-up management really work."

"I can certainly forward a memo from you about this to the executives under that label," Hugh said. "That's possible. But calling a meeting to talk about it is something I don't want to do, and I don't want you to do it, either. They'll wonder where we're coming from. They'll say that we don't have anything more practical to do than think of hair-brain ideas like becoming better at conflict. Productivity, innovation, customer service—yes; more conflict—no."

"But don't you see that's what we need to innovate, increase productivity, and serve customers? My group is going to be demoralized when I distribute the memo from the executive task force thanking them politely for their input on prices. We want a more general debate about pricing strategy, not a polite memo and then a bland statement about the need to keep reviewing the policy."

"We know, Eric, that you feel strongly about this, and that's why we agreed to have this meeting," Wendy said. "It's not so much that we disagree with you—we like your zeal—but we just know what's politically possible and what's not. Perhaps, though, we could push the executives a little. We could send them some articles to read. You never know, they might read them and be more open to your idea, Eric."

"We should get a real concrete article, nothing too theoretical, with lots of examples," Hugh said.

"The best would be a case study of a telecommunications company that appeared in an engineering magazine," Wendy said with a smile.

"Hearing things like that makes me question just how innovative the management really is." Eric began to regret putting his feelings so harshly as soon as the words left his mouth.

"These are conservative people running this company," Hugh said, trying to sound conciliatory.

"You might be as conservative, too, if you were running such a large company with so much to lose," Wendy said to Eric.

"And so much to gain," Eric replied.

"Rome wasn't built in a day," Hugh said.

"But in today's world, do we have as much time as we used to?" Eric asked.

"Sometimes it's best to wait things out. If you had been here as long as I have, you would have seen this company go through cycles of centralization followed by decentralization. Each new leader wants to make his mark by moving us in a direction different than his predecessor. I'm not sure we're any better off because of all that commotion."

"But managing conflict is not going away. We have to do it whether we are centralized or decentralized, have four or fourteen layers," Eric said.

"You always have conflict, I guess," Hugh said. "But it's so emotional and personal that I'm not sure that it can be or even should be taught."

"We shouldn't try to improve how we manage conflict because it's so important?" Eric asked without sarcasm. "That argument doesn't stand the light of day. How else are we supposed to get better at something so pervasive as conflict without some ideas and practice?"

Wendy nodded and Hugh said, "Perhaps so." They could see Eric's point, but they also wanted to move on from contemplating the abstract and long-term to something more practical. "I have some long meetings to get ready for," Hugh said. "So, Eric, send me that memo and perhaps with Wendy you can find a good article or two for the executives. Don't get discouraged. Take the long-term view."

"I can do that," Eric responded. "I'm glad we had this meeting even if it doesn't result in much action. Thanks for hearing me out."

"Don't mention it," Hugh said. "That's our job."

"You should be promoted over me," Eric said to Willem, with a mix of humor and irritation. "I don't think I'm cut out to be a flack-catcher." Eric summarized his meeting with Hugh and Wendy.

"But you're glad you asked for that meeting?" Willem had suggested that Eric meet with Hugh and Wendy after he had come in angry about the executive committee's memo on pricing.

"I'm glad I had an opportunity to express my views. Now I know more about NorTel and our leadership, but I'm also more disillusioned."

"Willem's first law of working at NorTel: don't expect too much and you won't be disillusioned."

"But it's so clear to me that we could profit a great deal if we really got serious as an organization about cooperative conflict."

"Was it so clear to you months ago, before we started experimenting with it?" Willem asked. "You took time, the company will take time."

"But we were ready to read, discuss, and practice. It wasn't just time. If they won't consider it, we can't get started."

Willem was sympathetic. "The guys running this place are engineers who are used to thinking that there's one right answer to every problem and if anyone can find those answers, they will. They're the winners who came out on top, so they must be right. The people below them are the losers and couldn't possibly have better ideas. Managing conflict doesn't fit easily into their thinking."

"I guess they're just smart enough to think that they can make the important decisions themselves."

"Eric, the company *will* learn to deal with its conflicts better. That's the future, but it may not be soon. In the meantime, we can enjoy ourselves, and you can try some things that may get the idea in front of the executives."

"I will do those things," Eric said. "But they seem so little, so minor compared to what could happen."

"Perhaps yes, perhaps no. Your team and mine can keep practicing and getting better. Maybe if the executives see us working at it, they'll get inspired."

"Stranger things have happened. How about that squash game we've been talking about?"

Using Conflict to Change an Organization

Eric was angry. He thought that the bland memo from the executive pricing task force had wronged him and his team. They had worked hard to develop ideas and a proposal that the task force had dismissed apparently without adequate justification.

With Willem's help, Eric saw this conflict as an opportunity to press for organizational change. NorTel could use conflict more openly and cooperatively to formulate a pricing policy that would give the company a strong internal focus and a consistent image with customers. To reach such a strategy required the full, conflict-filled participation of groups within NorTel. On their own, the executive committee could only act rashly or propose more drift.

Using Resistance

Conflict management is needed to change an organization, just as it is needed to create other changes. Whether the program is to reduce organizational layers, centralize or decentralize, or use mainframe or desktop computers, people will debate its value, practicality, motivation, and timing. These debates, even if the boss pushes the program through, affect its implementation and success.

Traditionally, dissent and questions about an organizational program have been considered "resistance to change" and the management has worked to overcome this resistance. People are accused of not wanting to change and of irrationally trying to hold on to the status quo.

From a cooperative conflict perspective, debates about an organizational program are an inevitable, natural aspect of making the many decisions necessary to implement change. Through these conflicts, people can examine, modify, and gain commitment to an effective, appropriate plan. Resistance is not so much to be overcome as it is to be used.

Eric wanted a full discussion of the value and practicality of NorTel becoming more conflict-positive. Unfortunately, top executives and managers resisted a full discussion. Eric's situation underlines a predicament in a conflict-positive change. The inability of an organization to manage its conflicts makes it difficult for it to consider a cooperative conflict program open-mindedly.

Thinking of the Long Term

Although NorTel managers were unwilling to discuss Eric's idea thoroughly, the company was not completely closed to influence. Eric was using his conflict skills to move NorTel toward considering such a change. Hugh and Wendy were listening to Eric's convictions and arguments. Some executives would read articles on conflict management and observe Eric and Willem's efforts to become more conflict-positive.

Eric wanted a full debate soon in which he, executives, and others would confront the rationale for investing in conflict management and wrestle with its implications. But he had to settle for indirect ways to consider such a program. Eric would have to take a long-term view in managing his conflict over the value of a cooperative conflict program.

Becoming a Learning Organization

Managing conflict is fundamental to organizational renewal. Without cooperative conflict, the organization has great difficulty considering and implementing change. With it, the organization can more adequately probe the value of restructuring or other change programs and create a program that fits its character and opportunities. The capacity to manage conflict is the basis for an organization's ability to learn, adapt, and change.

Becoming More Conflict-Positive

Once managers and employees become committed to improving their conflict management, what would a program for making NorTel more conflict-positive look like? The particular shape and timing would depend very much on the personalities and values of the people at NorTel and the demands and opportunities of their situation. They would have to work together to move away from conflict-negative ideas and habits to form a cooperative conflict team and organization.

Organizational members can begin by familiarizing themselves with cooperative conflict to understand how it is an alternative to viewing conflict as a competitive fight over opposing interests. They can review the research basis for cooperative conflict summarized in this and other books. They can clarify their confusions over cooperation, conflict, and competition. They can gain a clearer understanding of how open, skilled discussion enhances cooperative relationships, productivity, and innovation.

Then people can commit themselves publicly to managing their conflicts openly and cooperatively. While realizing that they cannot transform their ways of working overnight, they can credibly convey that they are motivated to learn cooperative ways of managing conflict. In this way, they can see each other as direct, open-minded, and responsive people who want to manage their differences.

They can follow this commitment with action to put cooperative values, procedures, and skills in place. The people at NorTel would decide the norms, allocation of rewards, and training needed to support their cooperative handling of conflicts. They would find resources that describe procedures and processes they could use to develop their skills.

People should strive for ongoing development and improvement. They can study cooperative conflict, rededicate themselves to learning, and help each other refine their abilities and skills. Learning to manage conflict is an continuous journey, not a one-stop trip.

For example, a fish farming company discovered that it needed to manage its conflicts cooperatively because it was facing a tough business environment. The founder thought his company could get rich quickly by growing fish in the waters off British Columbia. But the price for fish did not continue to rise, though the costs of paying for the excessive investments and feed did. Everyone needed to operate efficiently and effectively to reduce costs to make the company viable. Farm managers could not be allowed to hire more employees to supplement ineffective ones. Employees could not be allowed to waste expensive feed.

The new CEO described his vision of a conflict-positive, lean organization. He pledged to be direct and honest with the farm managers, distributed budgets and future projections, and told them that only if they were effective could the company succeed. The fish farmers read and discussed cooperative conflict and teamwork and quickly saw how they were critical to improving organizational and individual effectiveness and job security.

After reading, the farm managers brainstormed ways that they could establish and use cooperative conflict. They developed a companywide bonus plan to help them feel more cooperative. They improved how the farm managers communicated with each other via radio. They assigned several managers to one team and scheduled times when they could discuss issues face to face.

Several months later, they reviewed cooperative conflict, practiced team problem-solving skills, and evaluated the success of their plans. They were confident that they were developing the spirited teamwork critical for meeting the challenges of an unforgiving market.

Becoming more conflict-positive is often easier before tough difficulties and challenges emerge. A medical testing company's task force on developing a new computer system had a workshop on cooperative conflict soon after it was formed. By studying and discussing cooperative conflict, task force members publicly recognized that they would disagree and that their differences could be quite useful for designing a system that worked for the various groups in the company.

They developed rules and norms for how members of their group would deal with their differences. They were also able to allay suspicions they had about each other. The nurses and lab technicians heard and saw firsthand that the supposedly arrogant computer specialists were quite willing to listen and wanted a system that served their "customers." Task force members very much enjoyed the comraderie and stimulation of their group, and the company got a system that was on time and lived up to expectations.

Moving Toward the Future

NorTel's executives found the idea of cooperative, constructive conflict strange and readily dismissed any proposal that they should invest in developing the company's ability to manage conflict. New technology and training in technical skills seemed much more promising investments. Yet cooperative conflict is an idea whose time is coming. Today's organizations have too many conflicts and too many demands for change to brush aside strengthening their conflict abilities.

Contemporary Pressures

Ongoing improvement is a necessity for organizational survival and prosperity. There can be no illusion that the status quo is good enough. In the fiercely competitive marketplace, companies must continually improve the quality and delivery of their products or be overtaken by aggressive rivals.

Organizations must innovate under continual pressure. Whereas industry leaders once could afford the luxury of years, even decades, to develop and market a product, they must speed new products and new improvements to the marketplace. Once in the marketplace, new products are soon copied. Industry leaders then must upgrade their products and services.

Customers expect high-quality, innovative products to be served with their interests and needs in mind. Chemical companies, for example, are moving away from assuming they are selling a commodity product to considering themselves as serving their customers' needs for chemicals. They are trying to establish constructive relationships with customers, understand their problems, work with them to find solutions, and respond to their concerns. To serve customers in this way requires a great deal of constructive conflict and teamwork.

In addition to dealing with the conflict that is part of change and adaptation, organizations are facing increasing diversity in their makeup. Professionals and specialists trained in their own areas and disciplines are needed to operate complex technology and solve contemporary problems. Marketing, sales, production, and research and development are asked to work together in new product teams and task forces. Because of immigration and increasing numbers of women and minorities in the workforce, North American companies will be more and more racially, ethnically, and sexually diverse.

Management Innovations

Many managers are taking up the challenges to innovate and change. They are instituting participative management to involve employees in helping the organization change. Semi-autonomous work groups have the responsibility to manage themselves and produce a product. Hierarchies are being squashed and management layers reduced to lower costs and improve quality. Managers are structuring their organizations around markets to focus on serving their customers.

Although Eric doubted that NorTel's executives felt any urgency to change the company, they were trying to find new ways to manage. They were experimenting with "bottom-up management," pay-for-performance incentive schemes, and elaborate performance appraisal systems. Given their background, they could not easily understand the central importance of productive relationships. They assumed that an organization is composed of individuals and that the way to improve a company is to make each individual more able and motivated.

The executives did not clearly appreciate that the way to improve the abilities and motivation of individuals is through developing strong team relationships. To make participative bottom-up management and other innovations work, managers and employees must develop intensely cooperative goals and the abilities to manage their conflicts. Then they can put their different specialities, orientations, and opinions together to make participative management meaningful and to help the organization improve quality and serve customers.

Contemporary forces are smashing traditional bases of security for people and organizations. It is less and less tenable, even in large, well-known companies, to believe that people will have life-time employment and that the organization is guaranteed customers and income. Rather than security based on assumed stability, true security for organizations and for people increasingly will be attained by developing the capacity to use conflicts to respond and channel change.

NorTel's executives were also skeptical of conflict management because they did not have a plan to improve it. They saw themselves as practical, busy people who did not have time to consider lofty, abstract ideas. But, as the next chapter describes, managers have practical ways to encourage learning to manage conflict cooperatively.

Using Conflict to Change an Organization

Guides for Action

- Encourage an informed debate on how the organization should manage conflict.
- Provide books, articles, and examples that describe cooperative conflict.
- Debate the value of cooperative conflict for the organization and its people.
- Use available opportunities to influence others.
- Show how cooperative conflict can help the organization innovate, become more productive, and serve customers.
- Use cooperative conflict to develop a cooperative conflict program so that the means and ends reinforce each other.

- Commit publicly to managing conflict cooperatively.
- Work together to put cooperative conflict values and procedures in place.
- Strive for ongoing improvement.

Pitfalls to Avoid

- Expect everyone to agree that learning to manage conflict is a high priority.
- Treat dissent as obstruction.
- Expect change overnight.
- Conclude that because people do not want to improve conflict management now, they will not in the future.
- Moan that people are too closed-minded because they do not agree to a cooperative conflict program.
- Push through a conflict program despite resistance.

11

Teams to Support Learning

Our organization is based on mutual respect: The contributions of each person are essential to our success. We have learned that creating a business (or a product) depends on people who care about each other and about the customers we serve. This caring for one another translates into integrity in our operating system. We live up to our commitments. ...We share the fun, excitement, and triumph of group and individual success. We have pride in our accomplishments. We do it together, and we're the best in the business.

—Maria Straatmann, Computer Technology and Imaging

"Am I going to have to look at Mr. Grump-Face for another evening?" Carol said directly to Eric.

Eric managed a weak smile. A few weeks ago he would have reacted more strongly to Carol's anger, but now he understood that her anger was not being used against him. He was more relaxed and open to her feelings and more at ease expressing his feelings with her and at work. "What ever happened to the supportive partner theory?" Eric returned her teasing challenge.

"I'm the modern type. You'd better shed your nineteenth-century ideas if you expect to get by in the twenty-first."

Eric said seriously, "I'm disappointed I couldn't get through to Hugh and Wendy on that conflict program."

"You gave it a good shot. It's not your fault that they didn't go for it. As you say, 'The customer decides whether to buy, not me.'"

"The difference is that I have to live with this customer."

"You have other customers. What's your saying? 'The best cure for losing one sale is to find a customer for another one.'"

"At least someone's been listening to me."

"Hey, cut it out, Eric. I get annoyed when you get down on yourself. You exaggerate things so. It's not healthy."

"I do have the sales force. They should be more willing customers."

"Helping them get better at working together would be fun, I bet. More fun than trying to impress executives already impressed with themselves."

"Maybe I should do something."

"Use me as a sounding board. I've got some ideas."

After discussing with Carol and Willem his desire to help salespeople learn together, Eric read a chapter on how to strengthen conflict management abilities. He wanted to describe his vision of them becoming a team whose members would help each other get the job done and strengthen each others' conflict and cooperation skills.

"I've learned a great deal about working together, managing people and myself, through the idea of cooperative conflict," Eric began the meeting with his group. "The idea has helped me at work and at home and to understand NorTel as an organization.

"I'd like to find a vehicle for you to think more about your relationships and your conflicts. If we all could work as a team, the company would benefit from higher-quality work. You could also develop your abilities to work and live together, and we can all get better at that. Perhaps someday all of NorTel will join us, but for now we can help ourselves become more effective. Any questions?"

"Maybe many. I'm not sure I know enough to ask questions," Nick said. "Give me a picture of what we would actually do."

Eric replied that he saw them developing a formal group with regular meeting times and procedures. They would have two tasks: the first, to help each other get the sales job done; the second, to help each other improve their sensitivities and abilities to work together and manage conflict.

"Aren't we pretty good at working together as a team?" Nick asked. "We help each other. We have a few differences of opinion, which is only to be expected."

Eric did not want to pressure or coerce them. He wanted them to be committed to making this team successful. So instead of counterarguing, he asked Leslie and Rudy for their reactions. Rudy agreed with Nick, but he also thought that the group might be useful for dealing with conflicts with NorTel people outside the department.

"Listening to Eric, I was thinking that we could improve the way we handle conflicts with customers," Leslie said. "Those can be particularly sensitive."

"Do we want to focus just on managing conflict?" Nick asked. "Shouldn't we be talking about relational marketing, setting a climate, closing a deal, followup, dealing with a paranoid customer. We can all learn more about those things."

"That's conflict management, right? It's all part of managing conflict and establishing relationships," Leslie said.

"We have to develop strong cooperation and discuss issues and problems with customers," Eric said.

"Another question . . . I guess I'm being a devil's advocate," Nick said.

"Good. You're helping us understand and be more specific. And I need help getting specific," Eric laughed.

"How are we supposed to do this all?" Nick continued.

"There's a chapter here that I recommend you all read on learning conflict skills. It says that you need both ideas and experiences."

"I don't have any experiences managing conflict, but fortunately my colleagues do," Leslie deadpanned.

"With such an understanding boss, I can see where you don't have many conflicts," Eric joined in.

"Does that book say anything about dealing with a conflict with a boss who thinks he's understanding?" Rudy laughed.

After the laughter, Eric said, "In addition to experiences—which I can attest you all have—you need some good ideas and steps for resolving conflict so that you can analyze how you deal with conflict and plan how to improve. You already have an article on advocacy teams, and I can make some additional readings available that Willem and I found quite useful. So far so good?"

"Sensible, but a little abstract and general," Nick said.

"I should point out that Leslie and I are being very receptive to this," Rudy said with feigned seriousness.

"That comment brings me to my next point," Eric said with anticipation. "You'll have to develop strong cooperative relationships in which you can help each other understand ideas and steps to managing conflict. It's much easier and more fun to learn conflict together than by yourself. That I know. But as Rudy's comment nicely illustrates, this could be a most difficult task for you."

"I've got another question," Nick said. "Are we talking the three of us, or are you part of this team?"

"I hope I am," Eric said. "We're all going to have conflicts to manage and learn from. But I thought you three would want to meet often without me. I'm distracted with other issues and sometimes it's easier to talk when I'm not around. I have my own informal team that I've found invaluable for learning to manage conflict."

"To me, the first and decisive step would be for the three of us to get together and discuss whether we want to work together on this, if we want to have these cooperative, learning relationships you talked about," Nick said.

"If we are going to cooperate so much, then I think we'll have to make some changes," Leslie said. "As we've learned, our commission policy can get in our way. Sometimes we feel like we're working against each other."

"Perhaps that's where we should begin," Eric said. "After some reading, the three of you should list why working together as a team to get the job done and to improve your conflict skills would be valuable and important to you. You can also list the problems and shortcomings of working as a team.

"If you decide that developing strong, productive cooperative relationships is valuable, you can discuss how. Then all four of us can meet to see where we are and plan how we can do what we decide is best for us."

Learning Teams at Work

Eric had come to understand that cooperative team relationships are critical for developing conflict management skills and many other types of learning. Through conflict and reflection with Anthony, Willem, Carol, and others, Eric was learning about himself and managing conflict. It also made sense to him that working cooperatively is more productive on complex tasks than working alone or competitively.

How could Nick, Leslie, and Rudy work together to strengthen their conflict and other cooperation abilities? Direct, cooperative discussion and debate help people learn the theory of cooperative conflict. Understanding the link between cooperative relationships and open conflict and how cooperative conflict is useful for getting many things done require active involvement and debate. Criticisms and doubts need to be voiced so that people come to appreciate and understand the value of cooperative conflict.

Learning teams foster professional discussions in which people talk directly and honestly about the challenges, frustrations, and opportunities of working together. They talk in increasingly concrete and precise terms about the nature of cooperative conflict and how it can be applied. They use their shared, precise language to describe effective relationships and how they can be useful for implementing new technology, serving customers, and carrying out other innovations. Through discussing, explaining, and teaching, they see how they can use conflicts to make more effective decisions and reduce costs.

Cooperative conflict can help learning team members reflect on their experiences in an open, useful way. People, of course, learn from successful experiences and affirmative feedback. They also learn a great deal from failures and mistakes in which they have fallen short of the ideal of cooperative conflict.

Learning team members observe and give each other feedback. Most managers and employees are unsure of their impact on others and believe that others are reluctant to be direct and honest. In addition to observing each other, team members can observe each other dealing with people and conflicts outside of the group and give an outside, informed perspective. Observation and feedback should be reciprocal to underline that everyone is helping everyone else learn. People need to be respectful and, when pointing out shortcomings and problems, to recognize that everyone has strengths and weaknesses and good and bad days.

People in a learning team together plan programs and activities to strengthen their abilities to work together. As they try new ways of conflict, they clarify their understanding of cooperative conflict and get the encouragement needed to experiment with plans. Discussions about the effectiveness of previous attempts suggest how they can modify their plans for future action.

Structuring Cooperative Learning Teams

In successful learning teams, people are convinced they have cooperative goals. They believe they are moving in the same direction and understand that what is good for one is good for all. They are part of one community, celebrate each other's victories, and share each other's defeats. They are also convinced that they should and can discuss their opposing views and positions openly and constructively.

Cooperative Goals

How can cooperative relationships be fostered? Telling people that they should cooperate is insufficient. The key is to provide overlapping, consistent evidence of cooperative goals and their benefits. Task-oriented, bottom-line people can use common goals and shared rewards; people-oriented employees can use supportive attitudes and sense of community; bureaucracy-oriented people can use tasks and roles to believe they are united in the pursuit of cooperative goals.

Eric challenged Nick, Leslie and Rudy to have an inspiring, common vision and a collaborative feeling. They would help each other learn to make their group more innovative and productive and improve their abilities. Their learning would help them become more open, flexible, and competent at work and at home. Eric talked of his conviction that the sales group would be much more successful in developing leads and closing sales if they used cooperative conflict.

Eric wanted the salespeople to see their shared goals and common aspirations, that they would either swim or sink together. In learning groups, all team members are expected to improve their skills and to help each other learn. They recognize that this task is difficult and challenging and that they need everyone's ability and support to accomplish it. The individual members will be more successful to the extent that they can give and accept advice and support. They can all learn more and be more successful as each member develops more insight and skill in managing conflict cooperatively. "Small wins," in which the team successfully achieves a number of well-defined objectives, develop confidence among the team members.

Open, warm, and mutually rewarding interaction reinforces cooperative goals. People trust those they know and suspect those who remain unknown. Team members can discuss their feelings and the values they consider important. Small talk about one's family and oneself develops personal, trusting relationships. Social gatherings such as Friday afternoon "beer busts" and Christmas parties encourage friendly interaction.

Shared rewards reinforce cooperative goals. Nick, Leslie, and Rudy believed that Eric would recognize and appreciate the increased leads and successful closings of sales of the team as a whole. They would be able to attend workshops and courses together. Each would receive a written recommendation that would go into their individual files; each would be complimented at performance appraisal for contributions to the team.

Learning teams can develop their common identity by devising and publicizing their own names and symbols. Team members focus on their common characteristics and backgrounds. Eric showed that he cared about the team by attending some meetings, served as an observer, asked for feedback and ideas, and inquired about the progress of the team.

Eric could have asked Nick, Leslie, and Rudy to negotiate a contract in which they explicitly accepted their commitment to help each other become more competent. To do this, they would agree to attend and participate in the team meetings and to use and reflect on their conflicts and relationships. Everyone would be expected to contribute, discuss their experiences, observe and give feedback, and be observed and receive feedback. Members would take turns providing resources, hosting the meeting, and supplying refreshments.

Team members celebrate their successes together. They publicly recognize concrete examples of progress and swap good news about each other. Peers cheering each other on through quiet recognition and noisy hoopla reinforce the vision and the persistence to overcome obstacles.

Observing and Giving Feedback

Helpful Norms

- We do not have to be perfect.
- It takes time to learn complex conflict and cooperation skills.
- We are here to improve our abilities.
- We don't take feedback as personal attacks.
- We are secure enough to give feedback.

Guides

- Recognize that you can learn about conflict management and teamwork by observing experienced and inexperienced employees.
- Make observation and feedback reciprocal.
- Ask the observed employee what he or she wants you to focus on.
- Give feedback on actions and performance, not personal competence.
- Separate the employee's personal worth from his or her success in managing conflict.
- Be concrete and practical.
- Communicate respect for the employee's abilities and motivation.

Open Discussion

Eric also wanted to encourage full exchange and discussion. Nick, Leslie, and Rudy could discuss readings as well as their specific conflicts to sharpen their understanding of cooperative conflict. They could debate the nature and value of cooperative conflict. When people discuss their concerns and opposing views, they develop a deeper and more concrete understanding of cooperative conflict.

People can discuss opposing views to create various ways to apply the cooperative conflict theory. One person's approach will not be the same as another's. How a conflict is managed depends upon the personalities of the players and the opportunities and demands they face.

Eric could help the team members overcome their initial reluctance to reflect on how the team is developing. The team members needed to examine their own relationships and deal with their frustrations with each other. He might ask one member to observe and give the team feedback so they could discuss conflicts and build upon their successes.

Ongoing Learning

To the extent that Nick, Leslie and Rudy were committed to learning and believed they had cooperative interests, they were prepared to make their learning group succeed. They needed to persist to learn. Together they needed to debate conflict theory, discuss how they could use it as professionals, reflect on experiences, give each other feedback, and use journals, questionnaires, and other activities to improve their conflict management and celebrate acquiring its complex skills and sensitivities.

Cooperative conflict theory guides the development of learning teams. Team members have the inspiring common goal of promoting each other's competencies in dealing with conflicts and other people. Others learn as one member becomes more able. As the more experienced person teaches the less experienced, the more experienced person learns, too. They accomplish this cooperative goal by debating the idea of cooperative conflict and teamwork, discussing problems in applying the ideals, and deciding how they can improve their abilities.

Many managers and employees assume they cannot invest too much in learning because of pressures to perform and meet quarterly profit targets. Research on cooperative conflict reminds us that effective performance and learning are two sides of the same coin. Structuring cooperative relationships within an organization is a doubly-powerful strategy, for it aids immediate and future productivity. Except in the very short term, learning reinforces productivity. The next chapter discusses how cooperative conflict helps us reconcile other apparently opposing values.

Forming Learning Teams

Guides for Action

- Discuss how working as a team results in feeling supported as people and effective as employees.
- Detail how working as a team pays off for the company.
- Speak directly about your desire to work together with employees.
- Define employee jobs broadly to include working together to improve their abilities, the quality of work life, and company effectiveness.
- Confront the assumed tradeoff between company and employee welfare.
- Have learning teams debate conflict theory and knowledge.
- Promote professional discussions about working together and managing conflict.
- Have employees reflect on their experiences.
- Encourage teams to observe and give feedback.
- Have employees together plan how to improve their abilities.
- Develop cooperative goals through overlapping evidence of a common vision, mutual goals, shared rewards, common identity, and open, warm interaction.
- Negotiate a contract describing mutual commitments and obligations.
- Foster cooperative conflict so that learning team members can hammer out difficulties and combine their ideas to learn.
- Celebrate mutual learning together.

Pitfalls to Avoid

- Let people fend for themselves.
- Assume that getting people together means they will support each other's learning.
- Believe only young persons can learn.
- Accept people's shortcomings as inevitable.

Coming Together

If civilization is to survive, we must cultivate the science of human relationships—the ability of all people, of all kinds, to live together, in the same world at peace.

—Franklin D. Roosevelt

"I feel more in balance, less pulled and tugged in different directions," Eric said, as he came downstairs from saying goodnight to the children.

Carol put her book down. She was enjoying seeing Eric become more self-reflective. "You seem more relaxed. Having the kids make up stories before they go to sleep has been great. And I like the family dinner conversations about their day and ours."

"I'm committed to making it home for dinner. I'm delegating more and the team wants to do more."

"It's good you're taking the time now. Before we know it, the kids will be big and gone."

"It's more than time. Before, I used to think family and work were two different worlds. I had to be tough-minded at work and soft-hearted here. I'm afraid I ended up aggressive at work and a patsy at home."

"We want you tender-hearted," Carol said supportively. She did not want Eric to get down on himself.

"True, but I have to be tough-minded here. We can't bring up our kids just by telling them yes all the time. I've given in too much under the guise of trying to be good to them. I gave them things rather than me."

"You've blown up at them, too," Carol said directly.

"A waste. What can kids learn when I'm screaming at them, other than perhaps that I'm a little crazy?"

"I agree, but you can't be perfect."

"I've given up trying to be perfect. I just want to be on the right track."

"Our tender-hearted son has not given up trying to be perfect," Carol said.

"That's been bothering me, too. I'm going to talk to Ron, ask him to explain why he's trying to be perfect. Perhaps I can show him how unnecessary and impractical it is, how it will needlessly frustrate and anger."

"That conflict will take a long time to manage. What's this about being aggressive at work?"

"I have conflicts to manage there, too. We have problems that must be addressed and difficulties to work out. But we have to do it as a team, as people who care about each other."

"But work is so different than home."

"We have different and more intimate issues than at work, but we still must manage conflict together."

Carol considered how her husband had been changing over the months. "I like your feeling good about yourself."

"I've been too tough on myself. Always trying to be on top, to win, to get every sale, and to have everyone like me all the time. That's impractical. I can't even please my family and friends all the time."

"You've got to assert yourself and let others assert themselves."

"Even help them assert themselves."

"It's not about winning over others, but winning with others," Eric said seriously to Anthony at the gym.

"How are you going to win our race *with* me, when I'm going to win the race *over* you?" Anthony teased.

"That's another problem. Life's not a race, something to work and pain your way through for some big prize at the end."

Anthony realized that Eric was in a reflective mood. "I remember, years ago, hearing you talk about how you were going to the top, you were going to be rich and powerful. I think that's about the time I fled on my world travels."

"I'm changing," Eric said, as if this might surprise Anthony. "I'm getting older, maybe even wiser."

"We might both have to grow up," Anthony smiled.

"The phrase that I keep thinking about is 'coming together.' Things that seemed to be struggling against each other now seem to complement each other."

"Sounds good."

"Take goals. I've always assumed you had to suffer if you were going to succeed. But now I see that if you're not having fun, what's the point? And you probably aren't going to succeed either."

"I can see that." Anthony did not want to disrupt Eric's talk.

"I feel less pressure," Eric continued. "Less pressure to be right, to be on top of things. Now I depend on others more, but I'm more relaxed to be myself."

"But you're still working hard. You're serious about your work."

"I'm still committed to my career. I plan to keep working hard but more in balance, with people rather than against them."

"Didn't Aristotle talk about the golden mean, of avoiding the extremes and finding a middle ground?" Anthony made a mental note to review Aristotle's *Nicomachean Ethics*.

"But I don't mean compromise and always being in the middle. Truth is seldom in the middle."

"I think Aristotle meant something like putting things together, not just compromising. How come valuable insights seem so hard to get and so simple once you have them?"

"People telling you is not enough. It seems like we have to find these out for ourselves."

"What about you? How did you get these insights?"

Eric thought for a moment. "In a word, fighting. Perhaps more than fighting. Talking and thinking about my conflicts with Carol and the kids, with the people at work. The two of us have had some good talks. Thank you."

"You're welcome," he smiled, trying to accept Eric's gratitude. "I've learned, too. I've finally decided I do want to get married, raise a family, and find a serious career. I want the fights, the struggles, the full catastrophe. It'd be fun."

"Sure will. You can learn a lot from kids."

"I bet."

"I'm glad you're going to grow your roots here so I have a ringside seat. You probably won't have to struggle as much as I did. You've learned some things living abroad."

"I've got lots to learn."

"I use to think fighting with colleagues and family were just hassles and obstacles and sometimes just awful ones. If they only would have let me have my way, life would be great."

"But they didn't let you have your way."

"Thank goodness. I wouldn't have learned much if they did."

"You've thought a lot about your conflicts." Anthony had not seen Eric reflect so seriously since his first troubled years at the university.

"You know, you can't get much done without good relationships and you can't have them without managing conflict."

"Relationships are all around us."

"I used to think that I could do things myself, and I'm afraid my relationships showed it."

"You've always been a sensitive guy, though."

"I still want to be sensitive, but less obliged to get approval. Sometimes I'm going to get others upset, and sometimes I have to do things that get them angry. Real friends can get angry with each other." Eric smiled and teased. "Why am I angry with you?"

"Whatever it is, get it off your chest now because I don't want it to spoil our beer afterwards." Anthony welcomed the break of laughter, but then he continued seriously. "You found that reading about cooperative conflict useful."

"It turned all my conflicts into glorious love-ins," Eric laughed. "Seriously, I began hoping to find a quick fix that would help me over the obstacles others put in my way. But I don't think there's any kind of magic edge like that, and thinking there is is part of the problem."

"I don't follow."

"Rather than really looking at my way of handling conflict and my goals and assumptions, I was trying to get a technique that would give me an advantage over others. Then I discovered I had to work cooperatively with others and level with them and even trust that they would speak their minds."

"Makes sense to me, Eric."

"Working in this cooperative conflict way is so common-sense yet so difficult at the same time. The idea is okay to talk about at annual dinners, but we up and coming managers just don't let it interfere with everyday life."

"I guess the more established top executives find it easier to be open and work together."

"Not in my company. If you want real give-and-take, you have to go down to the field crews working in the hinterlands. The farther you are from head office and the farther down the ladder, the more people really work together and manage conflict, I'm afraid."

"Sobering thought."

"It's a challenge, too. It would be good to be part of turning NorTel around so that people worked honestly together."

"But working together, cooperative conflict seems so obvious. Why would anyone want to operate in a closed, competitive way?" Anthony asked.

"I've wondered about that, too. But managers don't want to. If you ask them how they want to manage their conflicts, they'll say they want to do it openly, fully, and find win–win solutions. Understanding it enough to give it a high priority and then doing it are the stumbling blocks."

"Is doing it that difficult?"

"It requires insight and consistency. Managers will quickly give up and press for harmony. What they don't realize is that it's through conflict that we get to unity."

Anthony thought for a moment. "I've seen some terrible groups where people talked about cooperation and unity, but underneath there was a lot of hostility and gossiping. Awful. Yet managing conflict is so basic. We've been doing it since childhood. Managers can't all be bad at it."

"They're not. Some are very good, but managing people requires more than that. A good manager has to encourage and help others manage their differences. Many people who manage conflict well aren't able to explain and teach others. For most, managing conflict seems like a great unknown, a great fuzziness in the sky that some people have and others don't."

"You're saying people don't have specific ideas and skills to work together and manage conflict?"

"Right, and that makes them move to areas where they feel more confident, into areas where they believe they can make progress. These are practical, conservative people running most companies. They want to be sure that they're doing something that will make a difference."

"Isn't managing conflict practical?"

"Yes, but you have to have a clear picture of what it is and how to get there. The bottomline is that managers think it's much more sensible to invest in new computer technology than in conflict management."

"But don't you have lots of conflicts to manage when you put in a new computer system?"

"True. Here's another place where things come together. Investing in people's conflict management is investing in the organization's ability to get things done."

Anthony nodded. "I can see how practical people may find this conflict management idea too grand, too elusive."

"But conflict is so much an everyday thing, too. The challenge is to have people see how this broad idea can help them understand and manage their many concrete conflicts."

"And how can you do that?"

"Together, through discussion and debate and reflecting on experiences."

"So experience and ideas, theory and action, can come together too."

"Yes. When people come together."

Integrated Values

Cooperative conflict exposes the fallacy that conflict is inevitably a test of competing wills over whose way will triumph. Conflict can transcend such thinking to create mutual value. Rather than resolving a conflict in one way or the other, or even splitting it in the middle, conflict can spur the creation of new alternatives that promote the interests and incorporate the ideas of many. Cooperative conflict helps us appreciate our diversity within our commonality.

Challenging Either–Or Thinking

As Eric discovered, we can use cooperative conflict to break out of either–or thinking and assumed tradeoffs to forge an integrative view of working and living with others. We tend to divide the world: us versus them, right versus wrong way, career versus family, emotions versus rationality, productivity versus people, long-term versus short-term. Cooperative conflict challenges us to appreciate the whole as well as its parts.

Eric learned that in organizations and in knowledge there are few right and wrong answers. Solutions adopted one week may need to be revised the next week to move toward more effective, appropriate decisions. Theories must be continually challenged, refined, and extended.

No longer experiencing his family and work as two separate worlds, Eric was building bridges between them. What he learned about conflict at home, he could apply at work; what he learned at work, he could apply at home. He realized that both family and work require constructive conflict and that he required sustaining cooperative relationships.

Rational and Emotional

Managing conflict cooperatively demands emotional give and take as well as intellectual inquiry. People critique, question, and explore arguments, but they also are committed to their positions and react emotionally to opposing arguments and strategies. Involvement, love, and anger all affect the dynamics and outcomes of conflict. Rather than asking people to be unemotional, cooperative conflict shows how feelings can be developed, expressed, and integrated.

Perhaps the most irrational assumption we can make in managing conflict is that our antagonist should behave rationally and unemotionally. They should coldly calculate their rewards and costs of various resolutions and chose the one that maximizes their tangible returns. We should then be able to influence our antagonist effectively by promising rewards for their agreement to our desired resolution and threatening to punish noncompliance: "If you do what I ask, you will be rewarded," or "If you cross this line, you will pay." Then we shout that our opponent is crazy when he does not comply.

We cannot assume that our antagonists have the same calculations on the benefits and costs as we do but should accept that they have their own perspective and calculations. As conflict provokes strong psychological and emotional dynamics, we must recognize that feelings and intangible considerations of social face and self-respect affect our antagonists' and our own negotiations. Appeals to be unemotional only make dealing with feelings more difficult. The road to constructive conflict is to express anger skillfully and manage feelings so that our emotions help us explore problems and create mutually beneficial, rational solutions.

People and Productivity

Cooperative conflict integrates "tough" and "soft" approaches to form a contemporary style of leading and changing organizations. Cooperative conflict requires confronting problems and struggling to work through them. But it is also soft because it requires people to be respectful and sensitive to each other and to develop strong, trusting relationships.

Cooperative conflict promotes people and productivity. People feel empowered when they resolve their differences and demoralized when they cannot. The company benefits by higher-quality solutions and more effective procedures. Cooperative conflict is good for people's well-being and competence and good for a company's effectiveness.

Cooperative conflict shows the connections between the technical abilities of completing tasks, the interpersonal skills of working with others, and the organizational abilities needed to cope with the demands of the workplace. Eric was learning about quality assurance through his discussions with Willem. He was becoming more savvy about the values and styles of NorTel's executives through his conflicts with Hugh and Wendy. Nick, Leslie, and Rudy would learn a great deal about the technique of marketing and selling as their learning group reflected on conflicts and issues. Managing conflict is fundamental for learning to develop relationships, getting jobs done, and thriving in an organization.

Cooperative conflict is a basis for a comprehensive approach to changing organizations. Typically, managers focus on programs to improve quality, productivity, customer service, or the quality of work life or to reduce costs through fewer people or lower inventory levels. Thirty years of Japanese automobile manufacturing experience has shattered the assumed tradeoff between quality and costs and shown that productivity, quality, and worker commitment march together. Spirited teamwork has driven this impressive performance. Managers and employees, production and engineering staff have together confronted problems and hammered out ongoing improvements.

Individual and Group

Perhaps the most fundamental reconciliation that cooperative conflict offers is between the individual and his or her group and organization. The choice is usually posed as being for the self or for others, acting selfishly or altruistically. Although some situations require such a choice, many situations in organizations allow and promote working for mutual benefit. In cooperation, people have a vested interest in each other's success and encourage each other to act effectively. When they use and discuss their differences cooperatively, they all benefit by working together to reach goals.

Cooperative conflict melds the value of individuality with the power of group action. By combining their opposing views, ideas, and perspectives, people in cooperation take effective action. With cooperative conflict, individuality and freedom of expression very much contribute to the quality of group life and to the productivity of the organization.

Applying Theory Together

In many conflicts, people not only disagree but suspect each other's motivation and conflict management. They see the other as too arrogant to listen to them or too conniving to speak honestly. Yet they are unable to focus on these attitudes by discussing how they manage conflict for fear of making the conflict too probing and "personal." Rather, after fighting competitively, they tend to avoid the issue and each other.

When conflict partners together adopt a cooperative conflict approach, they see each other as open-minded and can focus directly on the specific conflict at hand. They are operating on the same wavelength, not in the unrealistic sense that they will always agree with each other, but in the realistic sense that they agree on the approach they will use to deal with their differences.

To develop this shared framework, they together probe into the powerful theory of cooperative conflict and experiment with the complexities of applying it. They learn cooperative conflict and together commit themselves to using it.

Continuity Within Change

Rapid changes in technologies and markets have smashed our illusion of a stable status quo. The constant in our lives is change, but the pace and direction of change are unpredictable. Organizations in the future will be much different than today's, but no one knows how quickly or in what specific ways this transformation will occur. We recognize that we need new tools to deal with change, yet we also yearn for a return to basic values from a simpler, less frantic past. Cooperative conflict links past values with contemporary requirements.

Cooperative conflict, though critical for channelling and keeping on top of change, builds on traditional values of honesty, respect, and acceptance. People speak their minds honestly, respect other opinions, and trust each other's motives. Cooperative conflict is a modern, convincing way to show respect for individuals and appreciation of their diversity. Yet people have been managing conflict cooperatively for tens of thousands of years. Cooperative conflict is an ancient practice needed for contemporary demands.

Cooperative conflict gives continuity in the stream of change. The conflict issues and partners that we face tomorrow will be different from those of today and yesterday, but our need to manage conflict will continue. While future conflicts will require new approaches and new solutions, we can find stability in managing them together to promote our common aspirations.

Putting Cooperative Conflict to Work

I have tried to portray cooperative conflict as an ideal that people can realistically strive for, not as an easily achieved quick fix. We and our conflicts are too complex to be resolved by a slick technique. Some of our conflict partners are mean-spirited and manipulative; some are too powerful to be confronted; some are too fearful to learn to manage conflict. Sometimes we are too arrogant or fearful. We must make wise choices about whether we and our partners have the resources, fortitude, and motivation to pursue cooperative resolutions; then we must create strategies appropriate for our situation.

Cooperative conflict contributes much to our well-being and competence and to our organizations' adaptability and effectiveness. We exercise our uniqueness and independence yet feel valued and accepted; we express ourselves emotionally but reach out to others; we elaborate our thinking as we incorporate new ideas. We keep ourselves fresh and our organizations innovative.

But cooperative conflict requires a great deal. Learning to manage conflict is a lifetime pursuit of together probing ideas and reflecting on experiences. It is an integral part of keeping in touch and adapting to change throughout our lives.

The divisiveness and fragmentation of today's families, organizations, societies, and international relations have reinforced the view of conflict as villain. Yet, ironically, conflict binds us together. We all have conflicts to manage and we are more successful when we and our conflict partners have learned to manage them cooperatively. Then we use our diversity to create a spirited, enhancing unity.

References and Further Reading

This book is built upon the ideas and research of many people, some of whose work is noted below. Interested readers can use these references to explore their specific interests.

Conflict in Organizations

Bazerman, M. H. & Neale, M. A. (1992). *Negotiating rationally.* New York: Free Press.

Chase, R. B. & Garvin, D. A. (1989). The service factory. *Harvard Business Review*, July–August, 61–69.

Cosier, R. A. & Schwenk, C. R. (1990). Agreement and thinking alike: Ingredients for poor decisions. *Academy of Management Executive, 4*, 69–74.

Cusumano, M. A. (1988). Manufacturing innovation: Lessons from the Japanese auto industry. *Sloan Management Review, 20*, 29–39.

Eisenhardt, K. M. (1989). Making fast strategic decisions in high velocity environments. *Academy of Management Journal, 32*, 543–76.

Eisenhardt, K. M. & Bourgeois, L. J., III. (1988). Politics of strategic decision making in high-velocity environments: Toward a midrange theory. *Academy of Management Journal, 31*, 737–770.

Farnham, A. (1989). The trust gap. *Fortune*, December 4, 56–78.

Janz, T. & Tjosvold, D. (1985). Costing effective vs. ineffective work relationships: A method and first look. *Canadian Journal of Administrative Sciences, 2*, 43–51.

Johnston, W. B. & Packer, A. (1987). *Workforce 2000: Work and workers for the 21st century.* Indianapolis: Hudson Institute.

Kouzes, J. M. & Posner, B. Z. (1987). *The leadership challenge.* San Francisco: Jossey-Bass.

Lax, D. & Sebenius, J. (1986). *The manager as negotiator.* New York: Free Press.

Conflict Theory and Research

Deutsch, M. (1990). Sixty years of conflict. *The International Journal of Conflict Management, 1,* 237–263.

Deutsch, M. (1980). Fifty years of conflict. In L. Festinger (ed.), *Retrospections on social psychology,* 46–77. New York: Oxford University Press.

Deutsch, M. (1973). *The resolution of conflict.* New Haven, CT: Yale University Press.

Deutsch, M. (1949). A theory of cooperation and competition. *Human Relations, 2,* 129–152.

Falk, D. & Johnson, D. W. (1977). The effects of perspective-taking and ego-centrism on problem solving in heterogeneous and homogeneous groups. *Journal of Social Psychology, 102,* 63–72.

Johnson, D. W. (1971). Role reversal: A summary and review of the research. *International Journal of Group Tensions, 1,* 64–78.

Johnson, D. W. & Johnson, R. T. (1989). *Cooperation and competition: Theory and research.* Edina, MN: Interaction Book Company.

Johnson, D. W., Johnson, R. T. & Maruyama, G.. (1983). Interdependence and interpersonal attraction among heterogeneous and homogeneous individuals: A theoretical formulation and a meta-analysis of the research. *Review of Educational Research, 53,* 5–54.

Johnson, D. W., Johnson, R. T. Smith, K. & Tjosvold, D. (1990). Pro, con, and synthesis: Training managers to engage in constructive controversy. In B. Sheppard, M. Bazerman & R. Lewicki (eds.), *Research in Negotiations in Organization,* Vol. 2, 139–174. Greenwich, CT.: JAI Press.

Johnson, D. W., Johnson, R. T., & Tiffany, M. (1984). Structuring academic conflicts between majority and minority students: Hindrance or help to integration. *Contemporary Educational Psychology, 9,* 61–73.

Johnson, D. W., Maruyama, G., Johnson, R. T., Nelson, D. & Skon, S. (1981). Effects of cooperative, competitive, and individualistic goal structures on achievement: A meta-analysis. *Psychological Bulletin, 89,* 47–62.

Lowry, N. & Johnson, D. W. (1981). Effects of controversy on epistemic curiosity, achievement, and attitudes. *Journal of Social Psychology, 115*, 31–43.

Maier, N. R. F. (1970). *Problem-solving and creativity in individuals and groups.* Belmont, CA: Brooks/Cole.

Pruitt, D. (1981). *Negotiation behavior.* New York: Academic.

Rahim, M. A. (1993). *Managing conflict in organizations.* Second Edition. Westport, CT: Praeger.

Robbins, S. P. (1974). *Managing organizational conflict: A nontraditional approach.* Englewood Cliffs, NJ: Prentice-Hall.

van de Vliert, E. & Kabanoff, B. (1990). Toward theory-based measures of conflict management. *Academy of Management Journal, 33* 199-209.

Smith, K., Johnson, D. W. & Johnson, R. (1981). Can conflict be constructive? Controversy versus concurrence seeking in learning groups. *Journal of Educational Psychology, 73*, 651–663.

Tjosvold, D. (1983). Social face in conflict: A critique. *International Journal of Group Tension, 13*, 49–64.

Tjosvold, D. & Johnson, D. W. (eds.) (1989). *Productive conflict management: Implications for organizations.* Minneapolis, MN: Team Media.

Cooperative Conflict Research in Organizations

Etherington, L. & Tjosvold, D. (1993). *Managing budget conflicts: A goal interdependence approach.* Toronto: Canadian Association for Management Accountants.

Tjosvold, D. (1991). Rights and responsibilities of dissent: Cooperative conflict. *Employee Rights and Responsibilities Journal, 4*, 13–23.

Tjosvold, D. (1990). Cooperation and competition in restructuring an organization. *Canadian Journal of Administrative Sciences, 7*, 48–54.

Tjosvold, D. (1990). Flight crew collaboration to manage safety risks. *Group & Organization Studies, 15*, 11–191.

Tjosvold, D. (1990). Making a technological innovation work: Collaboration to solve problems. *Human Relations, 43*, 1117–1131.

Tjosvold, D. (1989). Interdependence and conflict management in organizations. In M. A. Rahim (ed.), *Managing conflict: An interdisciplinary approach,*, 41–50. New York: Praeger.

Tjosvold, D. (1988). Cooperative and competitive interdependence: Collaboration between departments to serve customers. *Group & Organization Studies, 13*, 274–289.

Tjosvold, D. & Deemer, D. K. (1980). Effects of control or collaborative orientation on participation in decision-making. *Canadian Journal of Behavioural Science, 13*, 33–43.

Tjosvold, D. (1987). Participation: A close look at its dynamics. *Journal of Management, 13*, 739–750.

Tjosvold, D. (1986). Dynamics of interdependence in organizations. *Human Relations, 39*, 517–540.

Tjosvold, D. (1985). Implications of controversy research for management. *Journal of Management, 11*, 21–37.

Tjosvold, D. (1984). Cooperation theory and organizations. *Human Relations, 37*, 743–767.

Tjosvold, D. (1984). Effects of crisis orientation on managers' approach to controversy in decision making. *Academy of Management Journal, 27*, 130–138.

Tjosvold, D. (1982). Effects of the approach to controversy on superiors' incorporation of subordinates' information in decision making. *Journal of Applied Psychology, 67*, 189–193.

Tjosvold, D. (1974). Threat as a low-power person's strategy in bargaining: Social face and tangible outcomes. *International Journal of Group Tensions, 4*, 494–510.

Tjosvold, D., Andrews, I. R. & Struthers, J. T. (1991). Power and interdependence in work groups: Views of managers and employees. *Group & Organization Studies, 16*, 285–299.

Tjosvold, D., Dann, V. & Wong, C. L. (1992). Managing conflict between departments to serve customers. *Human Relations 45*, 1035-1054..

Tjosvold, D. & Halco, J. A. (1992). Performance appraisal: Goal interdependence and future responses. *Journal of Social Psychology, 132*, 629–639.

Tjosvold, D., Johnson, D.W. & Fabrey, L. (1980). The effects of controversy and defensiveness on cognitive perspective-taking. *Psychological Reports, 47*, 1043–10530.

Tjosvold, D., Johnson, D. W. & Lerner, J. (1981). The effects of affirmation and acceptance on incorporation of an opposing opinion in problem-solving. *Journal of Social Psychology, 114*, 103–110.

Tjosvold, D. & McNeely, L. T. (1988). Innovation through communication in an educational bureaucracy. *Communication Research, 15,* 568–581.

Tjosvold, D. & Weicker, D. W. (in press). Cooperative and competitive networking by entrepreneurs: A critical incident study. *Journal of Small Business Management.*

Tjosvold, D., Wong, C. L. & Lee, F. (1992). Managing conflict in a diverse workforce: A Chinese perspective in North America. *Small Group Research, 23,* 302-321.

Tjosvold, D. & Wong, C. L. (1992). *Cooperative conflict and coordination to market technology.* Paper presented to the conference of the International Association for Conflict Management, Minneapolis, MN, June.

Tjosvold, D. & Wong, C. (1991). *Goal interdependence approach to conflict in the buyer-seller relationship.* Paper presented to the conference of the International Association for Conflict Management, Amsterdam, June.

Wong, C. L. & Tjosvold, D. (in press). Goal interdependence and service quality in services marketing. *Psychology & Marketing Journal.*

Becoming a Conflict-Positive Organization

Tjosvold, D. (1993). *Teamwork for customers: Building organizations that take pride in serving.* San Francisco, Jossey-Bass.

Tjosvold, D. (1991). *The conflict-positive organization: Stimulate diversity and create unity.* Reading, MA: Addison-Wesley.

Tjosvold, D. (1991). *Team organization: An enduring competitive advantage.* Chichester: Wiley.

Tjosvold, D. (1989). *Managing conflict: The key to making your organization work.* Minneapolis, MN: Team Media.

Tjosvold, D. (1986). *Working together to get things done: Managing for organizational productivity.* Lexington, MA: Lexington Books.

Tjosvold, D. & Tjosvold, M. M. (1991). *Leading the team organization: How to create an enduring competitive advantage.* New York: Lexington Books.

Developing Conflict Skills

Fisher, R. & Ury, W. (1981). *Getting to yes.* Boston: Houghton Mifflin.

Johnson, D. W. (1991). *Reaching out: Interpersonal skills and self-actualization.* Englewood Cliffs, NJ: Prentice-Hall.

Johnson, D. W. & Johnson, F. (1991). *Joining together: Group theory and group skills.* Englewood Cliffs, NJ: Prentice-Hall.

Johnson, D. W. & Johnson, R. T. (1991). *Teaching children to be peacemakers.* Edina, MN: Interaction Book Company.

Johnson, D. W. & Johnson, R. T. (1989). *Leading the cooperative school.* Edina, MN: Interaction Book Company.

Johnson, D. W. & Johnson, R. T. (1987). *Creative conflict.* Edina, MN: Interaction Book Company.

Latham, G. P. & Saari, L. M. (1979). The application of social learning theory to training supervisors through behavioral modeling. *Journal of Applied Psychology, 64,* 151–156.

Ury, W. (1991). *Getting past no: Negotiating with difficult people.* New York: Bantam.

Anger

Averill, J. R. (1982). *Anger and aggression: An essay on emotion.* New York: Springer-Verlag.

Ellis, A. (1987). The impossibility of maintaining consistently good mental health. *American Psychologist, 42,* 365–375.

Johnson, D. W. & Tjosvold, D. (1989). Managing stress and anger in conflict. In D. Tjosvold & D. W. Johnson (eds.) *Productive conflict management: Implications for organizations,* 193–215. Minneapolis, MN: Team Media.

Tjosvold, D., Tjosvold, M. M. & Tjosvold, J. (1991), *Love & anger: Managing family conflict.* Minneapolis: Team Media.

Organizational Learning and Change

Argyris, C. (1991). Teaching smart people how to learn. *Harvard Business Review,* May–June, 99–109.

Argyris, C. & Schon, D. (1978). *Organizational learning.* Reading, MA: Addison-Wesley.

Coch, L. & French, J. R. P., Jr. (1948). Overcoming resistance to change. *Human Relations, 1,* 512–532.

Acknowledgements

This book is built upon the theories, research and inspiration of Morton Deutsch and David W. Johnson. I also thank Chris Argyris, Bob Baron, Max Bazerman, Robert Blake, Jeanne Brett, Peter Carnevale, Rick Cosier, William Donahue, Martin Euwema, Barbara Gray, Len Greenhalgh, Irving Janis, Boris Kabanoff, Rod Kramer, Roy Lewicki, Willem Mastenbroek, Keith Murnighan, Maggie Neal, Dean Pruitt, Hugo Prein, Linda Putman, Afzal Rahim, Jorn Rognes, Jeff Rubin, Jim Sebenius Blair Sheppard, Ken Thomas, Evert van de Vliert, Jim Wall, Richard Walton, Bill Ury, and many other capable researchers who have contributed to our knowledge of productive conflict management.

Many colleagues and friends have helped me understand how co-operative conflict can be applied to achieve important objectives. Mary Tjosvold and Margaret Tjosvold demonstrated many successful ways to manage conflict in our family and our family businesses. Evert van de Vliert, Vera Hoorens, and Beth Anderson offered additions and changes to strengthen the book. Jenny Tjosvold assisted in its research and writing; she, Jason, Wesley, Lena, and Colleen make learning to manage our family conflicts enhancing and enjoyable.

Groningen, The Netherlands
Vancouver, Canada
December, 1992

Index

Tjosvold, Dean.
Learning to
manage conflict :

HD
42
.T583
1993

5/2/99			